Living with Thorns

Living with Thorns

When God Does Not Change Your Circumstances

A Biblical Survival Guide

By Mary Ann Froehlich

Discovery House Publishers is affiliated with RBC Ministries, Grand Rapids, MI.

Discovery House books are distributed to the trade exclusively by Barbour Publishing, Inc., Uhrichsville, Ohio.

Interior design by Melissa Elenbaas

Library of Congress Cataloging-in-Publication Data

Froehlich, Mary Ann, 1955–
Living with thorns : when God does not change your circumstances : a biblical survival guide / by Mary Ann Froehlich.
p. cm.
Includes bibliographical references.
ISBN 978-1-57293-263-0
1. Providence and givernment of God—Christianity. 2. Consolation. 3. Suffering—Religious aspects—Christianity. I. Title.
BT135.F76 2009
248.8' 6—dc22

2009002939

Printed in the United States of America

Table of contents

Dedicated to precious family members
and dear friends
who are remarkable thorns survivors.

Acknowledgments

Many thanks to:

My friends at Discovery House, who brought this project to completion, especially Annette Selden Gysen, who not only shared her skills but a piece of her heart with me.

My husband, John, for his unconditional love and tangible support through many years of writing.

My mother, Maria, who is the most remarkable, courageous thorns survivor I know and continues to inspire me daily with her life.

Debbie Sawyer, for sharing her story and biblical insights with me and inspiring me to write about the topic of forgiveness.

PeggySue Wells, for her supportive writing friendship, years of tender loving care, and insights about forgiveness.

Janae and Ron Phillips, who have exemplified the courageous journey of living with thorns and personally encouraged me with their gift of compassionate friendship.

Steve Fretwell, for his helpful insights about faith in the book of Hebrews and Debbie Fretwell, for encouraging my physical and spiritual health.

Isabel Harrison, for her faithful friendship and Latin expertise.

Pat Haslet, Janice Orlando, and Christine Williams, dear friends who have modeled life lessons in rising above thorns.

I am especially indebted to and inspired by those individuals who have shared their stories and struggles with me through the years. When requested, I have changed their names or used first names to protect their privacy. For this reason, they are not listed in the acknowledgments. Sometimes I have combined similar stories into composites.

Thank you to every person who has shared his or her story about living with thorns with me.

Part 1 Living with Thorns

Circumstances do not make a man,
they reveal him.

—James Allen

introduction

There was given me a thorn in my flesh, a messenger of Satan, to torment me. Three times I pleaded with the Lord to take it away from me. But he said to me, "My grace is sufficient for you, for my power is made perfect in weakness."

(the apostle Paul in 2 Corinthians 12:7b–9a NIV)

God did not remove Paul's thorn. Do you live with a thorn that torments you?

Do you live with a circumstance in your life that God does not change, no matter how you've cried out to Him, how many prayers you've prayed, how many tears you've shed, or how hard you've tried to improve it? You live with permanent pain that may be emotional, relational, or physical. You may suffer from an estranged relationship, a chronic illness, a difficult marriage, depression, a struggle with your own or a loved one's addiction, the scars of an abused past, or other tough circumstances. You may live with multiple thorns in your life.

You have begged God to free you from your pain, yet it remains. Trite sayings like, "God always answers prayer; sometimes He says yes, sometimes He says no, or sometimes He says wait," offer no comfort. Another popular cliché is "When God closes a door, He opens a window." You are tired of trying to pry that window open. It seems to be painted shut.

You may live with private pain. Your thorn is not a secret, but it is inappropriate for public knowledge. Hopefully you have a trusted few confidantes with whom you can share your pain. Living alone with our struggles is the toughest road.

As Christians, we are enamored with the life-changing testimony, the success story. We want to hear about former prostitutes, skid row bums, or drug addicts who came to know Christ. Their lives are radically different now, and they have dynamic ministries, leading others to Christ. We love to hear them share their stories at Christian conferences. We want to hear about the couple whose marriage was headed for divorce before they both became Christians; now they enjoy a blissful marriage. We revel in these miracles of God. And they are miracles. But what if there is a deeper miracle that we are missing?

We may be overlooking the miraculous lives of those who live with visibly unchanged circumstances, the "less than success" stories. If you see yourself in this group, you are in good company. Many of God's followers throughout Scripture are our models. They cried out to God, too, and felt despair at what seemed to be God's silence.

This book will not address individual circumstances, such as improving your health, marriage, or family relationships. Books covering these topics abound. This is not a self-help book. While books like these can be inspirational and helpful, I am coming to the conclusion that they may not be biblical, because the focus is primarily on self. Striving for as near perfect life as possible on this earth is not the perfection in weakness that Paul describes.

This book is about the imperfect life. I have wrestled with this topic for many years, beginning when I worked with terminally ill children. My questions and grief led me on an in-depth biblical journey, searching the Scriptures for a definitive answer. Of course, I didn't find one. But hopefully this book based on my journey will offer you comfort, scriptural encouragement, and some tangible survival tools for facing those unchanged circumstances and fighting the resulting despair, weariness, fear, loneliness, and broken heart that often accompany our pain.

This book is divided into two parts. Part 1 assures you that no matter how difficult your circumstances are, you are not alone in your pain. Others have experienced your struggles. Jesus himself sympathizes with your weaknesses (Hebrews 4:15). Part 2 offers biblically based survival tools for living with your thorns. Questions are offered at the end of each chapter as more food for thought.

When I wrote *An Early Journey Home: Helping Dying Children and Grieving Families*, I came to the conclusion that theological arguments and questions like "If God is all powerful and all good, why does He allow His children to suffer?" or "Does God *allow* or *cause* suffering?" do not matter when a parent's child lies cold under a white sheet. Wrestling with mental exercises in trying to understand God's ways is not constructive. Learning to effectively comfort grieving families and ease their pain is helpful. *Living with Thorns* will offer you a similar approach for your own life.

More important than the question "why" is "who." Whom do we trust? Whom do we run to when life is unbearable? Peter Kreeft states it so well: "We are finally led not to the answer but to the Answerer."

The thorns that seem to hem us in are in reality placed there to close us in to God himself, to protect us from evil, to provide us with sanctuary in the midst of a troubled world.

—Margaret Clarkson

Adversity is the state in which a man most easily becomes acquainted with himself, being especially free from admirers then.

—Samuel Johnson

Character cannot be developed in ease and quiet. Only through experiences of trial and suffering can the soul be strengthened, vision cleared, ambition inspired, and success achieved.

—Helen Keller

Living with Thorns 1

Some people grumble that roses have thorns;
I'm just glad that thorns have roses.
—Marteau

Scholars wonder what Paul's pain was. In several translations of the 2 Corinthians 12:7–9 passage, Paul's struggle is described as a thorn in the flesh. *The New English Bible* describes it as a sharp physical pain. What is more important than the exact nature of Paul's pain is how he handled it. He asked God three times to remove it, and then he accepted it. He understood that God had a purpose for his pain. I handle my thorns quite differently. I plead with God repeatedly over years to remove them. Paul's thorn may have been a physical pain, but we understand today that our bodies and emotions are integrated in relation to our physical health. Paul lived with difficult circumstances and extreme stress.

Paul is not the only person in the Bible who was afflicted with thorns. The theme of thorns recurs throughout Scripture. Jesus wore a crown of thorns: "Then Pilate took Jesus and had him flogged. The soldiers twisted together a crown of thorns and put it on his head. They clothed him in a purple robe and went up to him again and again, saying, 'Hail, king of the Jews!' And they struck him in the face (John 19:1–3 NIV).

Think how profound the fact is that Jesus wore our pain, our thorns, to the cross. Jesus died to remove our sin. He died to remove the sting of the thorns, but the thorns remain in this life. I have observed throughout Scripture and in the lives of people I love that God protects us through our pain, but He doesn't eliminate it while we live on this earth. He uses it for His purposes.

Isaiah 7:23–25 (NIV) gives us a picture of a country infested with briars and thorns. Verse 25 states, "You will no longer go there for fear of the briars and thorns." In the parable of the sower, Jesus said, "Other seed fell among thorns, which grew up and choked the plants, so that they did not bear grain" (Mark 4:7 NIV). Our thorns have the potential to choke out our faith. But if we can find a constructive way to live with our thorns by trusting God, they may strengthen our faith and even enhance our lives. This is our challenge.

As you cry out to God to miraculously remove your thorn, you may be missing that the true miracle is *you*. God may not be changing your outward circumstances, but He is changing you at your core. The most powerful biblical image showing the purpose of thorns is given to the prophet Hosea: "Therefore I will block her road with thorn-bushes and obstruct her path with a wall, so that she can no longer follow her old ways. When she pursues her lovers she will not overtake them, when she looks for them she will not find them; then she will say 'I will go back to my husband again; I was better off with him than I am now' " (Hosea 2:6–7 NEB).

We have a jealous, passionate God who will do everything required to guard our relationship with Him.

Roses among Thorns

Debbie's father sexually abused her and her sisters, her mother physically abused them, and both parents emotionally abused them. Debbie's nightmarish childhood introduced her to deep despair. When she was a teenager, Debbie attended a local church, but she never told anyone there about her home life. The pastor and his wife took a liking to Debbie and asked her to babysit for their children, and soon Debbie was babysitting often and became part of their family. For the first time, as Debbie interacted with the members of the pastor's family, she observed how a healthy, loving family functioned. She understood the difference that Jesus Christ made in the lives of this family and in hers as well.

Even though many people's lives are strangled by thorns, I have repeatedly observed that God hears their cries and sends roses. Sometimes He sends a single rose put in an unexpected place, and other times He delivers a bouquet. In Debbie's case, God gave Debbie a rose when He used the pastor and his family to rescue her from a desperate situation. Today Debbie is a speaker and Bible study teacher, offering hope to women with a past similar to hers.

In the midst of our own struggles, perhaps we can be God's roses to other hurting people.

> Praise be to the God and Father of our Lord Jesus Christ, the Father of compassion and the God of all comfort, who comforts us in all our troubles, so that we can comfort those in any trouble with the comfort we ourselves have received from God. For just as the sufferings of Christ flow over into our lives, so also through Christ our comfort overflows. (2 Corinthians 1:3–5 NIV)

Food for Thought

- Think about the roses that God sent you during a difficult season in your life.

- When have you been a rose in a troubled person's life? Who have you comforted because of the comfort you have received from the Father of compassion?

- Reread 2 Corinthians 12:7–9. Paul says that his thorn is intended to keep him humble, and it is a messenger of Satan. To be honest, I understand these thoughts but am not comforted by them. Throughout Scripture, I see that God allows Satan to test and challenge God's people within the boundaries of His love and protection. I also know that God uses circumstances in our lives to make us more Christlike and build our spiritual character. What are your responses to this passage?

- Reread Hosea 2:6–7. When has God blocked your way with thorns so that your relationship with Him would be strengthened? If you were running away from God, did it cause you to run back to Him?

There is great pain and suffering in the world. But the pain hardest to bear is your own.

—Henri Nouwen

It is too simple to dismiss the book (Job) by saying it deals with the problem of suffering. It is a heart-rending account of a man in the depths of despair who cannot believe that God is punishing him.

—John White

The surgery of life hurts. It helps me, though, to know that the surgeon himself, the Wounded Surgeon, has felt every stab of pain and every sorrow.

—Philip Yancey

The sovereignty of God is the one impregnable rock to which the suffering heart must cling.

—Margaret Clarkson

Living with Despair 2

My soul is overwhelmed with sorrow to the point of death.

Mark 14:34 NIV

Webster's Dictionary defines *despair* as "an utter loss of hope or confidence," and complete despair is that feeling that there is no way out. In his book *In the Name of Jesus*, Henri Nouwen observed, "Beneath all the great accomplishments of our time there is a deep current of despair. While efficiency and control are the great aspirations of our society, the loneliness, isolation, lack of friendship and intimacy, broken relationships, boredom, feelings of emptiness and depression, and a deep sense of uselessness fill the hearts of millions of people in our success-orientated world." This kind of despair leads people to wonder if anyone loves them or cares. The close companion of despair is depression, which sometimes leads to suicide, the ultimate act of hopelessness. Victor Frankl, a psychiatrist and Holocaust survivor who experienced and witnessed tremendous suffering in a concentration camp, drew the conclusion that "despair is suffering without meaning."

The opposite of despair is hope, and a synonymous idea for hope is trust, to place confidence. Christians may certainly feel despair, but technically we cannot be overwhelmed by despair because our confidence, hope, and trust are placed in God. No matter how desperate our circumstances, we can trust in Jesus Christ.

The most well-known example of Jesus' despair occurred in the garden of Gethsemane. Jesus said, "My soul is overwhelmed with sorrow to the point of death" (Mark 14:34 NIV). Jesus cried out to God, asking Him to change His circumstances if possible: "*Abba*, Father, . . . everything is possible for you. Take this cup from me. Yet not what I will, but what you will" (Mark 14:35–36 NIV). Jesus understands our desperation.

Paul battled with despair as if it were an enemy, saying, "We are hard pressed on every side, but not crushed; perplexed, but not in despair; persecuted, but not abandoned; struck down, but not destroyed" (2 Corinthians 4:8–9 NIV). Paul experienced countless desperate situations, and he lists them in 2 Corinthians 11:23–28. They include torture, being shipwrecked and left in the open sea, constant danger from attackers, sleep deprivation, starvation, thirst, being cold and naked, and extreme pressure and stress. Wouldn't you feel despair if you had endured these difficulties?

Job felt despair and wanted to die. David felt despair. Jonah felt despair in the belly of the whale. Widows and barren women were often inconsolable with despair. The Israelites felt despair. In studying the Scriptures, I discovered that most of the major forces in God's story felt despair at some point in their lives. Besides sharing a feeling of despair, what they had in common was what they did with their despair. They cried out to God and He heard them, but He did not immediately change their circumstances. Sometimes God waited decades to bring relief, but other times people's difficult situations remained unchanged for a lifetime. Moses never entered the Promised Land. These heroes may have fully experienced and felt despair, but their hope and confidence were placed firmly in God.

> I would rather be choked outright;
> I would prefer death to all my sufferings.
> I am in despair, I would not go on living;
> leave me alone, for my life is but a vapour.
>
> (Job 7:15–16 NEB)

Despair Today

> Despair is to be without a future because you recognize the futility of the present.
>
> —Walter Wangerin

Karen met her future husband, Don, at the company where they both worked. He was fun, handsome, and could charm anyone. After they were married, Karen learned that Don was a binge drinker. Sometimes he would go to Las Vegas for the weekend, gambling, drinking, and enjoying women. He always returned remorseful, vowing that it would never happen again. Karen had become a Christian and did not want a divorce. She forgave Don and committed to do everything possible to make their marriage work.

Karen sought counseling. Don entered a rehabilitation program and began attending Alcoholics Anonymous meetings. Karen and Don became involved in a church with a supportive pastor and loving community. While Karen worked at a demanding job to support their two daughters, Don struggled with retaining employment. He also struggled with depression, guilt, and low self-esteem. Karen prayed that God would heal her husband from his addictions, and Don wanted God to heal him. Karen prayed that God would heal their marriage and protect their family. She trusted God and clung to Him, devouring the Scriptures. Her faith deepened through the darkness.

After peaceful periods, Don's binges would begin again. He would disappear and clean out their bank accounts and overcharge credit cards. With the help of counselors, Karen set strict boundaries. She put most of their money in accounts that her husband could not access, keeping him from using it for gambling. Karen knew that forgiveness did not mean tolerating abuse. She told Don that the next time he binged, their marriage would be over.

When his next binge came, Don disappeared for weeks. Then Karen returned home from work one day with her daughters to find broken glass and beer cans strewn all over her home. Don had broken the kitchen window with a sledgehammer. He left a note next to a butcher knife: "I didn't know if I would hurt you or me." He stole antique family heirlooms, other valuables, and the family dog. He even stole his daughter's money out of her room. It was the violent act of a desperate man. His desertion was final, and Karen never saw him again. Divorce was unavoidable with Karen's children's safety in jeopardy.

With the support of their church and caring friends, Karen and her daughters slowly began to put back together the pieces of their lives and heal. Karen said that the end of her marriage did not feel like an amputation but rather like having a limb ripped off in a violent accident. She was honest with her children about

Don's illness. She tried to see Don through God's eyes and extend His forgiveness to a broken man. Ten years after Don abandoned their family, Karen spoke with him on the phone, realizing that she truly had forgiven him.

Today Karen is remarried to Robert, a wonderful and loving man, and they have blended their two families. Don remains unchanged, a prisoner of his addictions.

> God never lets you down.
> But people do.
>
> —Francine Rivers

If you have felt despair in facing a hopeless situation, God's followers in biblical as well as current times know the pain you endure.

Depression

> Hopelessness and despair are the colors that depression wears. It cloaks me in them like a suit of clothes. Joy becomes invisible. I can only see joy's shadow. I can't touch it or remember what it feels like.
>
> —Carmen R. Rutlen

Despair and depression often dovetail. Chronic depression is a complicated illness, far beyond the scope of this book. I have struggled with a mild form of chemical depression linked to another illness, treatable with exercise and by managing the hormonal imbalances in my body. More severe forms of depression can require medication. Depression is not simply sadness and is often not a direct result of circumstances. My mother-in-law lost her youngest son and husband in a tragic accident. She has been incredibly sad in her life, but told me that she has never experienced depression. Sadness and depression can be two different conditions.

Some symptoms of depression include fatigue, a lack of energy and drive, feelings of hopelessness, a loss of appetite, excessive sleep or an inability to sleep, or frequent crying. The best description I have heard of depression is this: The world is in living color, but the depressed person's world is in black and white. Some people describe depression as a black cloud that descends and crowds out all joy or a veil that they cannot reach through. Others describe it as anger turned inwards. Depression coupled with despair can be debilitating. It feels like being stranded in a deep pit with no way to climb out.

In 17:7, Job says, "My eyes grow dim with grief, and my limbs wear away like a shadow" (TJB). Job states in 23:2, "My thoughts today are resentful, for God's hand is heavy on me in my trouble. If only I knew how to find him" (NEB). I think that Job understood despair and depression.

"Snap Out of It"

> A spirit depressed wastes the bones away.
>
> Proverbs 17:22b TJB

Sometimes people who have not experienced despair or depression can be intolerant of those who do suffer with these problems. These inexperienced people view despair and depression as weakness and, worst of all, sin. Sin is certainly brokenness, and each of us struggles with wounds and brokenness in different ways. Yet those who judge despair and depression as disobedience to God only heap guilt on an already paralyzed person. Advising someone to "snap out of it" is not helpful. The last thing that a struggling person needs is to feel judged. It was the last thing that Job needed. His former friends felt that his troubles were his own fault and probably the result of disobedience. Job answered, "How harsh are the words of the upright man! What do the arguments of wise men prove? Do you mean to argue about words or to sift the utterance of a man past hope?" (Job 6:24–25 NEB). Job was desperate and past hope.

Sorrow upon Sorrow

> So much in life is unpredictable, but God's love is certain.
>
> —Barbara Johnson

Paul states in Philippians 2:25–27 that his friend, Epaphroditus, was ill and almost died. Paul describes Epaphroditus as his brother, fellow worker, and someone who cared for Paul's needs—someone who was a good friend and important to Paul. Yet Epaphroditus did not die, and Paul says, "But God had mercy on him, and not on him only but also on me, to spare me sorrow upon sorrow" (v. 27 NIV).

Barbara Johnson knows what it is like to experience sorrow upon sorrow. Her oldest son was killed in action in Vietnam. Her second son was killed in an auto accident with a drunk driver. After her third son told Barbara and her husband that he was gay, they became estranged, and Barbara's son did not speak to her for eleven years.

Was God unmerciful? Did God not spare Barbara sorrow upon sorrow? Barbara encourages us: "Thousands upon thousands of people have 'been there'—seemingly at that point of no return . . . frozen . . . out of the flow. But then, sometimes suddenly, most often slowly, they get back on center, 'thaw,' inch from despair back to faith, and stand strong again under the waterfall of God's ever-flowing love."

Through her experiences of despair, Barbara Johnson has earned the right to say that we do not face a hopeless end but, rather, we have endless hope in Jesus Christ.

> He sends his word to bring the thaw
> and warm wind to melt the snow.
>
> Psalm 147:18 TJB

Food for Thought

> We do not want you to be uninformed, brothers, about the hardships we suffered in the province of Asia. We were under great pressure, far beyond our ability to endure, so that we despaired even of life. Indeed, in our hearts we felt the sentence of death. But this happened that we might not rely on ourselves but on God, who raises the dead. He has delivered us from such a deadly peril, and he will deliver us. On him we have set our hope that he will continue to deliver us, as you help us by your prayers. (2 Corinthians 1:8 – 11a NIV)

- Despair and hope are paired often in Scripture. In these verses from 2 Corinthians, Paul despaired even of life, yet he set his hope on God. Just as our actions cannot be brave unless we first know fear, perhaps we cannot know true trust and hope unless we experience despair. How have despair and hope played joint roles in your life?

- Have you experienced the despair of a hopeless end? When? Were you encouraged by endless hope? In what form did that hope come?

- We have already looked at Job's complaint in 23:2: "My thoughts today are resentful, for God's hand is heavy on me in my trouble. If only I knew how to find him" (NEB). Now read Job 23:1–6: Even though Job is desperate, he knows the truth and puts his confidence in God: "God himself would never bring a charge against me. There the upright are vindicated before him, and I shall win from my judge an absolute discharge" (Job 23:6b–7 NEB). It is during our darkest hour that we most need to tenaciously cling to the truth.

> Often trust begins on the far side of despair.
>
> —Brennan Manning

Loneliness is one of the hardest of pain's companions to learn to live with, but it is always present in sorrow or sickness.

No one else can know our loss or our heartache, sympathize as they will. Suffering is essentially within myself. To suffer is to be alone—utterly, completely alone.

But there is One who can enter into our pain—the solitary Man who was despised and rejected by man—a man of sorrows who was acquainted with grief.

—Margaret Clarkson

A sense of isolation enfolds me like a cold mist as I sit alone and wait at life's shut gate. Beyond there is light, and music, and sweet companionship, but I may not enter.

—Helen Keller

Living with Loneliness 3

A father to the fatherless, a defender of widows,
    is God in his holy dwelling.
God sets the lonely in families,
    he leads forth the prisoners with singing;
    but the rebellious live in a sun-scorched land.

Psalm 68:5–6 NIV

Robert was an only child who never married or had children. His parents, aunts, and uncles are now deceased. Robert lives his life alone, but he is not lonely. He is rich in friends, active in his church, enjoys a meaningful career, and fills his life with productive activities. He has become "Uncle" Robert to many of his friends' children.

Megan is separated from her abusive husband and estranged from her parents. She is raising her four children alone. Katie is married to an emotionally distant man who works long hours, travels for business, and ignores her when he is home. Susan enjoyed a happy fifty-year marriage until her husband developed Alzheimer's disease. She cares for him at home with the help of a part-time nurse. Most days he does not recognize her. While Megan, Katie, and Susan do not live alone, they feel lonely and isolated.

God tells us in Psalm 68:5–6 that He becomes our family and frees us from our prison. The *Jerusalem Bible* translation states in verse 6: "God gives the lonely a permanent home, makes prisoners happy by setting them free, but rebels must live in an arid land." The verse is intended to celebrate the idea that God is the companion of those who are lonely, yet many lonely people understand verse 6 in a different way. Sometimes the loneliest people *do* live in families. They feel like they have been set in families to be lonely. This type of isolation, this feeling of being disconnected from the people we are supposed to be closest to, can feel like solitary confinement.

Job experienced this intense loneliness. When his life fell apart, everyone he knew, from his wife and siblings to acquaintances and friends, abandoned him (Job 19:13–19).

> To my wife my breath is unbearable,
> for my own brothers I am a thing corrupt.
> Even the children look down on me,
> ever ready with a jibe when I appear.
> All my dearest friends recoil from me in horror:
> those I loved best have turned against me. (Job 19:17–19 TJB)

If you struggle with loneliness, you will also understand Paul's feelings of abandonment in 2 Timothy:

> Alexander the metalworker did me a great deal of harm. The Lord will repay him for what he has done. You too should be on your guard against him, because he strongly opposed our message.
>
> At my first defense, no one came to my support, but everyone deserted me. May it not be held against them. But the Lord stood at my side and gave me strength, so that through me the message might be fully proclaimed and all the Gentiles might hear it. (2 Timothy 4:14–17a NIV)

During his imprisonment after his arrest, Paul wrote this letter to Timothy. Even though Alexander has harmed him, Paul is more hurt that everyone deserted him. He is not only alone in prison but feels lonely and forgotten. Yet Paul tells Timothy that God didn't leave him; He stayed by his side. Paul also sees the big picture of God's plans: the Gentiles have heard Paul proclaim God's message, though he stood alone.

Jesus knew loneliness in the garden of Gethsemane (Mark 14:32–41 NIV). The disciples were physically with Him, but they were not emotionally with Him. Jesus was at His lowest point, "deeply distressed and troubled." He was "overwhelmed with sorrow." The disciples could not stay awake and keep watch with Him. Jesus tried to wake them three times and then announced, "Enough! The hour has come." He seemed to say, "I give up. It's too late."

It is interesting to note that Paul asked for his thorn to be removed three times, and Jesus asked His disciples three times to stay awake with Him. Then He stopped asking.

The psalmist often cried out to God about his feelings of isolation. He describes his loneliness as a prison:

> Thou hast taken all my friends far from me,
> and made me loathsome to them.
> I am in prison and cannot escape;

my eyes are failing and dim with anguish.
I have called upon thee, O Lord, every day
and spread out my hands in prayer to thee. (Psalm 88:8–9 NEB)

Thou hast taken lover and friend far from me,
and parted me from my companions. (Psalm 88:18 NEB)

David is a hunted man, expressing his desperation in psalms 142 and 25:

I look to my right hand,
I find no friend by my side;
no way of escape is in sight,
no one comes to rescue me.
I cry to thee, O Lord,
and say, 'Thou art my refuge;
thou art all I have
in the land of the living.' (Psalm 142:4–5 NEB)

Turn to me and show me thy favour,
for I am lonely and oppressed.
Relieve the sorrows of my heart
and bring me out of my distress.
(Psalm 25:16–17 NEB)

Have you experienced times in your life when you felt lonely, oppressed, and abandoned by friends and family? Did you feel that God was all you had in the land of the living? If you did, you have a strong bond with many of our biblical heroes.

A Different Kind of Miracle

Paul wrote several letters from prison, including Ephesians, Colossians, Philippians, and Philemon. Paul states in Philippians 1:13 (NIV) that "it has become clear throughout the whole palace guard and to everyone else that I am in chains for Christ. Because of my chains, most of the brothers in the Lord have been encouraged to speak the word of God more courageously and fearlessly." Note how clearly Paul addresses the issue of fear.

Paul is imprisoned while he is writing the book of Philippians, yet the theme of his letter is joy. When Paul and Silas first visited Philippi, they were miraculously freed from jail when a violent earthquake shook the prison doors open (Acts 16:22–40). We too want our prison doors to fly open and our chains loosed. Yet Paul and Silas did not leave the jail but stayed to witness to their jailer, who became a Christian. The next day Paul and Silas were released from prison and escorted out of the city. They were rescued. Paul has experienced no such miracle as he later writes his epistle to the Philippians.

Paul has experienced a deeper miracle. He tells the Philippians that he has "learned to be content whatever the circumstances." He now knows "the secret of being content in any situation" (Philippians 4:11–12 NIV). Our culture equates contentment with happiness, but the two are radically different. Being content is defined as being satisfied, with limited wants or desires. In contrast, the state of happiness is often dependent on pleasurable circumstances and having our desires met. Paul is fully satisfied with Jesus Christ. He states, "I can do everything through him who gives me strength" (Philippians 4:13 NIV). Paul knows contentment and deep joy though he is physically restrained in a jail cell, facing possible execution. The greater miracle is that Paul is now rescued while *in* a prison cell instead of being rescued and released *from* a prison cell.

Cultural Loneliness

> It is no longer the case that machines are an extension of our needs. On the contrary, we are extensions of the imperatives of machines.
>
> —Chuck Leddy

The battle against loneliness is becoming tougher to fight. Beyond our personal prisons of relational heartache, we are affected by a society that breeds isolation. In our technological age, many people would rather have relationships with machines than people. We can access most experiences through a screen (such as televisions, computers, or cell phones). Some people certainly prefer having relationships with people through machines rather than in person. Social networking Web sites continue to grow in popularity. An online life is sometimes more convenient than an actual one. Pornography addiction, chat-room relationships, and the Second Life phenomenon are extreme examples of how people show a preference for machines over other human beings.

A recent Duke University research study revealed that Americans have decreased their number of close friends. One-fourth of polled Americans reported that they had no one to talk with about important issues. Unmarried adults are becoming a majority in our country, where married adults were once the majority.

Psychologists and educators are legitimately concerned that children who grow up in this culture have learned that distanced relationships are normal. A study released by the Henry J. Kaiser Family Foundation revealed that children and teens spend an average of six and a half hours per day involved in screen-related activities. Today's young people have been labeled the "plugged-in generation."

Whether our loneliness is the result of wounded relationships or a wounded society, we know that God can relieve the sorrows of our heart and bring us out of our distress (Psalm 25:17).

> Our children are being raised by appliances.
>
> —Bill Moyers

Food for Thought

- How have you experienced the difference between being alone and feeling lonely? Have you experienced loneliness in your own family?
- Have you ever remained in a "prison of loneliness" to be a witness to others as Paul and Silas did? What were your circumstances, and how were you able to live out the gospel?
- Has our society's technological immersion affected your feelings of isolation? If so, in what way?
- Which biblical model's struggle with loneliness do you most identify with: Job, Paul, Jesus, or David? Why do you feel an identity with that person? Even though you may feel completely abandoned, as each one of them did, what assurance do you have that you are not alone?

> Loneliness didn't come knocking, or greet me at my window. She didn't make an appointment, or call to chat about the weather. One day I discovered her right next to me in bed.
>
> —Swathi Desai

Peace will never come until we have accepted in totality all that is involved in our suffering, even facing and accepting the fact that the sorrow that has struck us so suddenly may never be removed. Acceptance is taking from God's hand absolutely anything He chooses to give us, looking up into His face with love and trust.

—Margaret Clarkson

Every adversity carries with it the seed of an equivalent or greater benefit.

—Napoleon Hill

Living with Weariness and Illness

4

Be still, and know that I am God.

Psalm 46:10 NIV

Living with thorns is most challenging when it involves our physical bodies. Physicians frequently hear common complaints of exhaustion, stress, and fatigue. As a society, we are a weary people. If we are weary, we are exhausted in strength and endurance. We are simply worn out.

Struggling with illness presses us harder. We may live with frequent mild illnesses, brought on by prolonged stress; endure serious chronic pain or illness; or face life-threatening illness. Sometimes we don't know the cause of our ailments. Is it fatigue, depression, illness, or despair? Which is the cause, and which is the effect? Most doctors agree that our physical health and emotional/mental health are interrelated. Scientists have found that chronic stress weakens the immune system and accelerates aging in cells.

All we know is how hard it is to get out of bed every morning. We wonder why God doesn't heal us. If we believe that God is able to heal us, we then question why He chooses not to heal us.

Sharon, an abuse survivor who you will read about in chapter 5, suffers from debilitating migraine headaches that send her to bed for days. Linda, who was also abused by her father, lives with chronic fatigue syndrome and fibromyalgia. Abuse survivors often experience physical pain and other symptoms into adulthood, the lasting effects of childhood trauma, similar to post-traumatic stress syndrome. Why doesn't God free Sharon and Linda from their physical and emotional pain?

When Justine was hospitalized several times with chronic ailments, she learned later that her husband abused their children during her absences. They are now divorced. Why did God not heal Justine or protect her children during her illness?

Sometimes the church adds to our pain. When Christina's daughter became comatose during a biopsy procedure because of the doctor's error, she never regained consciousness. Christina's church strongly believed in healing, and church members prayed for months that Christina's daughter would be healed, often at her hospital bedside. When she did not recover and eventually died, the church turned their back on Christina's family. Philip Yancey says about the church: "Many suffering people want to love God, but cannot see past their tears. They feel hurt and betrayed. Sadly, the church often responds with more confusion than comfort."

Dan is a chaplain who suffers from severe chronic back pain and has endured multiple surgeries. Kevin is a pastor who has been hospitalized several times with intestinal problems, and his doctors are baffled by his illness. Amy Carmichael, a missionary in India, was bedridden for twenty years, enduring constant pain. She wrote twenty books, including *Rose from Brier*, letters to encourage the ill. Patty was once an active church organist and pianist, but today she is crippled with arthritis and is unable to play either instrument.

You may live with your own serious illness. If not, you probably know people who suffer from chronic illness, live with cancer or other life-threatening diseases, experience daily severe pain, or have experienced traumatic accidents. Our frail human bodies can deteriorate or be injured in multiple ways.

Inside-Out Truth

The most important key to living with thorns, especially physical ailments, is understanding how our culture has insidiously seeped into our faith. Biblical truth is upside down, inside out, diametrically opposed to what our culture teaches and values. Our culture prizes health, productivity, efficiency, accomplishment, and visible success. While these things are not inherently wrong and can be pursued in a positive way, they can also be destructive to our souls if we idolize them. We will do almost anything to avoid physical or emotional pain.

During a recent visit to my daughter's church, I noticed a young college student signing during the worship service. She was practically dancing. My daughter explained that this young woman had come to know Jesus Christ after a difficult time during her teen years. She had a beautiful singing voice and received a music scholarship to attend a respected conservatory in a university. She became involved with the worship team in her local church. She passionately worshiped and served God with her voice. During her junior year, the doctor found a growth on her vocal cords. She was never able to sing again. She lost her music scholarship but stayed at the university with the help of a grant. She now worships God through using sign language, singing in her soul.

Logic dictates that if God were to heal some of the people mentioned in this chapter, they would be much more useful to Him in accomplishing His purposes. Nothing could be further from the truth. Sometimes we make the mistake of viewing God through our culture's eyes, as if He were our boss. Here are truths we can glean from Scripture that contrast with our culture's workaholic values.

- God is not an employer. Imagine that you are running a business and interviewing potential employees. You are going to select the best qualified candidate with the most impressive background. You want the best person for the job. That's not how God works. Throughout Scripture and the present day, God often selects the least able or qualified candidates to accomplish His work. He chose Moses, David, Joseph, Paul, prostitutes such as Rahab, and countless others who would not have had the best credentials or even wanted the job.

- Effective business managers remove obstacles from their employees' paths so they can be productive and accomplish the most possible. God is a different kind of leader. He often puts obstacles in our path so that we learn to trust Him.

- Managers evaluate their employees' performance and reward them with bonuses or raises based on their ability to reach set goals and be successful. God is unimpressed with our performance, and He is uninterested in our success. What He prizes most is our relationship with Him.

God is our father, not our boss. Christ is our beloved. We are God's precious children, His adored bride. God does not work in our lives to make us more productive but to bring us closer to Him. The Mary versus Martha syndrome rings true today, in major companies as well as churches. Jesus did not value Martha's workaholic patterns but did appreciate Mary sitting at His feet. Wasting time is viewed as one of the worst sins in our culture. God is more concerned with who we are than with what we do.

Looking through our culture's eyes, we may feel useless when we are sick, fatigued, or unable to function well. If we are not visibly useful to God, then what good are we? Yet God sees our physical weakness as an opportunity for us to completely focus on Him without distraction. C. S. Lewis said that pain is God's megaphone. One woman explains her experience with God's megaphone:

> Two years ago I fractured my lower back. I was in physical therapy for a year, and thankfully most of my motor function has returned. But I have had to learn to live with chronic pain. Some days are worse than others. I am not sure why, but sometimes the pain becomes so intense. I am frustrated and feel betrayed by my body. I have trouble sleeping at night and require pain medication. I live with the fear that I will become addicted. So often I wonder why God permitted this to happen to me. Was it His severe protection from some choice I would have made if I were healthy? Sometimes I feel that He has deserted me to suffer alone. I do not feel angry toward God, but I often feel abandoned. I do not like to talk about this struggle with pain. Yet I am more compassionate toward other suffering people. During my life, I have had to interact with three family members who were mentally ill. Today I better understand physical and emotional pain. I've learned that God is sufficient in the midst of our circumstances. He feels my pain, hears my questions, sees my struggles, and listens to all my complaints. He is faithful, and I can trust Him. My greatest hope is in eternity, where I will no longer have the pain of

this world but will bask in the presence of the one who suffered so much for me.

Held Up by God

> Yahweh will go in front of you,
> and the God of Israel will be your rearguard.
>
> Isaiah 52:12b TJB

Isaiah 52:12 is one of my favorite verses. God goes before us to lead the way, and He comes behind to hold us up. A few years ago I asked my doctor about my fatigue and unusual lack of energy, symptoms of a chronic condition I've had for thirty years. My regular medication did not seem to be helping. The doctor kindly explained to me, "I can help to regulate your body within normal levels, but I can't change you into someone else." This was the plain truth of the matter. Though I imagined what my life could be and what I could accomplish if I felt healthier and had boundless energy, if I were "someone else," that is not who God created me to be. When I am too exhausted to forge ahead, He leads the way. Every day He holds me up.

Joni Eareckson Tada called the accident that left her a quadriplegic a "glorious intruder." Without it, she says she would have probably lived a comfortable life with little purpose. Yet which of us would choose to receive this glorious intruder or have one of our children experience it?

Food for Thought

- Do you have a "glorious intruder" in your life? Have you lived with chronic pain or illness? Does fatigue weigh you down?

- Have you struggled with feeling useless to God, as you measure yourself against the world's standard of worth? If so, read the following verses, understanding that God cares for you when you are ill or weary:

> Blessed is he who has regard for the weak;
> the Lord delivers him in times of trouble.
> The Lord will protect him and preserve his life;
> he will bless him in the land
> and not surrender him to the desire of his foes.
> The Lord will sustain him on his sickbed
> and restore him from his bed of illness. (Psalm 41:1–3 NIV)

The *New English Bible* states in Psalm 41:3 that God turns down our bed. He nurses us when we are ill. He also protects us when we are weary. God gives us strength when we are tired and weak:

> The Lord is the everlasting God,
> the Creator of the ends of the earth.
> He will not grow tired or weary,
> and his understanding no one can fathom.
> He gives strength to the weary
> and increases the power of the weak.
> Even youths grow tired and weary,
> and young men stumble and fall;
> but those who hope in the Lord
> will renew their strength.
> They will soar on wings like eagles;
> they will run and not grow weary,
> they will walk and not be faint. (Isaiah 40:28b–31 NIV)

We live lives that are hopelessly broken and we know it.

—Paul Tillich

It is a simple fact of life: there will be difficulties, setbacks and disappointments. For some people there will be rejection; for others there will be tragic losses. For still others there will be inexplicable suffering. No one is immune from pain; it is part of the package that comes with life.

All people will experience the brokenness of the world intersecting with their lives in a thousand and one ways.

—Gordon T. Smith

Living with a Broken Heart 5

My days have passed, far otherwise than I
had planned,
and every fiber of my heart is broken.

Job 17:11 TJB

After teaching her morning Bible study, Liz returned home to find a note left by her husband. He had packed his things and left. Liz never saw this coming; she was blindsided. She and her husband had been married twenty-five years, raised children, and been active in their church. Later she would learn that her husband had become involved with a female co-worker in his office.

Liz hoped for reconciliation, but her husband pursued a divorce. During the first weeks of her initial shock, Liz experienced chest pains so severe that she went to the hospital. She thought that she was having a heart attack, but instead her heart was breaking.

Scientists recently have named this experience stress cardiomyopathy, or broken heart syndrome. The symptoms are similar to a heart attack but do not normally cause permanent damage. Older women are the majority of sufferers. Severe sadness and shock can create high levels of stress hormones, catecholamines, in our bloodstream, which may affect the heart. Patients have trouble breathing and feel intense pain.

Depression and loneliness have also been linked to heart disease. Different from cardiomyopathy, these extended experiences can have long-term effects. Suffering a broken heart is a true phenomenon, and it is centuries old.

> The Lord builds up Jerusalem;
>   he gathers the exiles of Israel.
> He heals the brokenhearted
>   and binds up their wounds. (Psalm 147:2–3
> NIV)

Our Lord is the doctor of our souls. God knows us at our core because He created our fragile minds and bodies. Isaiah tells us that he came to heal the brokenhearted.

> The Spirit of the Sovereign Lord is on me,
>   because the Lord has anointed me
>   to preach good news to the poor.
> He has sent me to bind up the brokenhearted,
>   to proclaim freedom for the captives
>   and release from darkness for the prisoners.
> (Isaiah 61:1 NIV)

We may experience a broken heart through rejection or betrayal by a spouse, parent, or child. Our hearts may feel broken due to a traumatic loss. We grieve our own brokenness. This pain is the offering we lay on the altar: "My sacrifice is this broken spirit, you will not scorn this crushed and broken heart" (Psalm 51:17 TJB).

God understands and is tender with our broken hearts. He is the perfect parent who wraps His arms around us and never lets go as we weep.

> Put your head on the chest of God and weep.
>
> —Nicole Johnson

Weeping in God's Arms

> I have no food but tears, day and night;
> and all day long men say to me,
> "Where is your God?"
>
> Psalm 42:3 TJB

Have you ever felt like the psalmist, crying and feeling abandoned by God? Scripture teaches us that when we cry, God sees our tears. Psalm 56:8 says that God records and stores every tear in His flask or wineskin. Hezekiah lay dying, weeping and pleading with God. Isaiah 38:5 tells us that God heard Hezekiah's prayer, saw his tears, and added fifteen years to his life. God hears us when we cry.

Jesus was overcome with emotion and wept when He saw Mary, Martha, and their friends weeping over Lazarus' death. John 11:33 states that Jesus was "deeply moved in spirit and troubled" (NIV). Initially Jesus tries to comfort Mary by explaining that because

He is the resurrection and the life, Lazarus will rise again. Mary understands but remains inconsolable in her grief. Then Jesus goes to the tomb and calls Lazarus out. I don't think that Jesus can stand to watch His friend Mary endure so much pain. God is moved by our tears and anguish.

Crying caused by deep emotion releases different chemicals from lubricating tears or reflex tears that react to an irritant. Emotional crying is one way that our bodies dispose of toxic substances. It is cathartic, cleansing us from tension and distress. God intends for us to cry as a way to heal our pain. Jeremiah 31 is especially revealing about how God understands and responds to the tears of His people. God is our escort and our comfort, ultimately replacing our sorrow with joy.

> They come home, weeping as they come,
> but I will comfort them and be their escort.
> (Jeremiah 31:9a NEB)

> I will turn their mourning into gladness,
> I will relent and give them joy to outdo their sorrow.
> (Jeremiah 31:13b NEB)

> Cease your loud weeping,
> shed no more tears;
> for there shall be a reward for your toil,
> they shall return from the land of the enemy.
> (Jeremiah 31:16 NEB)

A Paralyzed Heart

> Every tear we shed becomes his tear.
> He may not yet wipe them away, but he makes them his.
>
> —Peter Kreeft

Sharon's heart was so deeply broken that she could not feel the pain, and, as an adult, she could not cry. Sharon was a good mother and longed to be able to cry with her children, feel a wide range of emotions, and stop living with a feeling of numbness. Only when she began to pull back the layers of abuse she had endured as a child did the tears come.

Sharon grew up knowing that she was a "mistake," the pregnancy that forced her father to marry her teenage mother. When Sharon's brother was born three years later, she learned that he was the prize, while she could barely be tolerated. Sharon's parents were verbally and emotionally abusive to her and one another. As their marriage deteriorated, they each had affairs. Sharon learned to stay out of her father's way to avoid his anger. Any negative emotions, especially crying, were not tolerated. Sharon did everything she could to please her father, but she couldn't find the key to his heart. When she brought home a report card with straight A's, he refused to look at it.

Sharon's parents started leaving her home alone at age eight to care for her five-year-old brother. Her mother would be gone for hours, sometimes overnight, only leaving a note with a list of chores for Sharon to complete. Sharon often didn't know where either of her parents was. Now she knows that she and her brother were abandoned so that her parents could pursue their extramarital affairs. When she was ten years old, her father left their family. She had no way to contact him and seldom saw him. On one rare weekend visit to his apartment, Sharon's father tried to molest her but stopped when she froze in terror.

Sharon's mother continued to see her lover, Carl. Now Carl was hugging Sharon in ways that didn't feel right to her. Sharon tried to tell her mother, but she wouldn't listen. Soon Sharon's mother married Carl.

Carl was Sharon's new stepdad, and he was also an alcoholic. When Sharon was thirteen years old, Carl's hugs became fondling. When Carl's brother came to visit, he would even enter Sharon's bedroom and touch her in inappropriate ways. Sharon's mother suspected something but did nothing. She was either at work or asleep.

By age 15, Sharon had nightly visits from Carl for sex. When she became pregnant, he took her to have an abortion and continued to sleep with her. When Carl was unemployed, he would be waiting for Sharon when she returned from school. Sometimes he would become angry and slap her.

Carl and Sharon's mother divorced after four years of a turbulent marriage. When Sharon's mother was a young teen, she had been sexually abused by her own stepfather. Their relationship had produced a son, who was given up for adoption. Sharon's mother was so wounded that she couldn't protect her daughter or face the truth. Her own mother had not protected her.

Sharon left home when she was eighteen years old. Her mother gave her a set of luggage for her birthday and said, "Take the hint."

Sharon later married and had her own family. She has been a fierce protector of her daughters' safety. When Sharon's mother, who remarried again, wanted her granddaughters to come for weekend visits, Sharon asked her, "Can you guarantee that my daughters will not be molested?" Her mother started to cry and said no. Sharon declined the weekend visits. Her mother became angry and did not speak to her for years. Sharon's husband developed a mental illness and displayed abusive behavior later in life, a result of his own childhood traumas. They are now separated.

Through hard work and determination, with the help of counselors, Sharon has chipped away at the wall inside her. Healing is a lifetime process, but now she can cry and feel different emotions. She no longer survives life as a numb robot. She has been willing to feel the painful emotions to experience the good ones. While her biological father punished her for tears, she knows that God is the parent who accepts and loves His children when they cry.

If my father and mother desert me,
Yahweh will care for me still. (Psalm 27:10 TJB)

The Father's Comfort

When you weep and feel that your heart is breaking, God is listening. He comforts you as a parent comforts a child:

> Like a son comforted by his mother
> will I comfort you. (Isaiah 66:13 TJB)

> Enough for me to keep my soul tranquil and quiet
> like a child in its mother's arms,
> as content as a child that has been weaned. (Psalm 131:2 TJB)

> In the wilderness, too, you saw him: how Yahweh carried you, as a man carries his child, all along the road you traveled on the way to this place. (Deuteronomy 1:31 TJB)

No matter the depths of your distress or grief, regardless of the messages you received in your childhood, you can cling to the biblical image of God, your loving parent, who holds you, carries you, and comforts you. God may not immediately change your circumstances, but He does promise to immediately wrap His arms around you and console you.

> I need only say, "I am slipping,"
> and your love, Yahweh, immediately supports me;
> and in the middle of all my troubles
> you console me and make me happy. (Psalm 94:18–19 TJB)

> For I, Yahweh, your God,
> I am holding you by the right hand;
> I tell you, "Do not be afraid,
> I will help you." (Isaiah 41:13 TJB)

Views of God

Sharon's numbness and inability to feel God's loving arms around her are common responses among those who have suffered childhood abuse at the hands of their parents, the two people that a child should be able to completely trust. Viewing God as a father is not a comforting image for abuse survivors. Sharon understands intellectually through reading Scripture that God is her loving father. She holds fast to these passages, but she cannot feel the love of a parent. Her only associations and memories are that parents are toxic, neglectful, and abusive. They abandon you, use you for their own pleasure, or ignore your needs.

Sharon experienced severe migraine headaches as a young child and continues to have them as an adult. Her mother would ignore her when she had headaches and refused to comfort her by holding her, rocking her, or even bringing her an aspirin or a cold drink. How can Sharon feel God's arms around her?

Sharon cannot feel God's love or imagine that He values her. She understands and clings to scriptural truth with her mind. Yet when Sharon reads her Bible, she feels that she is reading love letters written to someone else. She tells me that it feels like reading someone else's mail.

Author Elizabeth Dewberry was abused by someone outside her immediate family. In *Fiction and Faith*, she explained her struggles:

> When I was writing *Break the Heart of Me,* I had to come to terms with the fact that I was molested as a child . . . It rocked my faith pretty severely, of course. I grew up believing in a God who would never give me more than I could bear. Then I realized that all the time I had been believing that, I was being molested. It reshaped the way I understood the world.

Childhood abuse does rock its victim's faith to its core. Sharon has often asked, "Why didn't God protect me from those horrors?" She tries to give her children a healthy vision of God's love and protection through her care for them, not wanting them to experience her pain. The greatest gift a parent can give a child is a glimpse of God our father. We are not perfect parents, but He is. People who have felt deeply loved, protected, and cared for by their parents are more able to internally understand a relationship with God, their loving father. It is a natural response. The greatest miracles are those people who feel God's love without having any earthly models. Even greater miracles are parents who love and protect their children when they did not receive that love from their own parents. Friends and counselors have told Sharon that she is a walking miracle, a mother who trusts God and fiercely loves her children, despite feeling so unloved as a child. She is beginning to grasp that truth.

> Then the Lord God will wipe away the tears from every face
> and remove the reproach of his people from the whole earth.
> The Lord has spoken.
>
> Isaiah 25:8 NEB

Food for Thought

- Think about how your relationship with your parents prepared you for your relationship with God the Father. This will be a comforting exercise for some, a painful exercise for others. What messages do you communicate to your own children about God as our parent?

- Compare these translations of Psalm 56:8:

Enter my lament in thy book,
  store every tear in thy flask. (NEB)

You have noted my agitation,
  now collect my tears in your wineskin! (TJB)

Record my lament;
  list my tears on your scroll—
  are they not in your record? (NIV)

In Old Testament times, professional mourners saved their tears in bottles. How do you now feel about shedding tears, knowing that God your Father sees and records every one? Are you comforted to know that God is deeply moved when you cry?

A time for tears,
A time for laughter;
A time for mourning,
A time for dancing.

Ecclesiastes 3:4 TJB

Those who went sowing in tears
now sing as they reap.
They went away, went away weeping,
carrying the seed;
they come back, come back singing,
carrying their sheaves.

Psalm 126:5–6 TJB

Experiences of crying and mourning are often juxtaposed with experiences of joyful dancing and singing throughout Scripture. The time for sorrow here on earth will someday be washed away by heaven's joy. Yet we also experience these miniature seasons in our own lives. Reflect on those seasons when you experienced great sorrow and weeping and ways that God later "gave you joy to outdo your sorrow."

> When words are most empty, tears are most apt.
>
> —Max Lucado

The world is hip-deep in tears. Compassion is not an option. It is a matter of survival.

—Sue Monk Kidd

Christ reveals that God is deeply affected by us, passionately responds to us and suffers incredibly for and because of us.

—Gregory Boyd

The case against God can be quite simply put like this: How can a mother trust and love a God who let her baby die?

—Peter Kreeft

Living with Fear 6

I seek Yahweh, and he answers me
and frees me from all my fears.
Psalm 34:4 TJB

Mary Ann was always a fearful child. Beyond normal childhood fears, she felt oppressed, imagining the worst that could happen in any situation. She was thirteen when her dad died from lung cancer, and then her worst fears were confirmed. While her older siblings returned to a normal life, Mary Ann retreated to her room and cried for months. She was terrified that her mom would also die. She couldn't verbalize her fears.

As an adult, Mary Ann has clung to biblical truth, knowing that God does not give her a spirit of fear. Yet her battle with fear can still paralyze her. When her children went on school trips, she worried about their safety and feared the worst. When her husband pursued activities that did not include her, she feared that he would find someone else because she had been through a serious break-up in high school. When she had breast lumps and endured a lengthy diagnostic process, she was overwhelmed, believing that she had cancer like her dad. But Mary Ann did not have breast cancer.

When fear grips her, Mary Ann compares the experience to a frog being slowly boiled in water. Any initial worry may seem innocent, but in time she is consumed with terror. She realizes the root of her fear is that she can't control all her circumstances—only God can.

God has not removed Mary Ann's fear, but He has given her scriptural truth to combat it. She must deliberately trust God when she feels the water beginning to boil.

> The Lord is close to those whose courage is broken
> and he saves those whose spirit is crushed.
>
> Psalm 34:18 NEB

Sometimes our worst fears come to pass. Before going to sleep, Patrick prayed nightly for his children's safety. One night while he was praying, his teenage son died in a car accident. The following night and many nights after, Patrick struggled, not knowing how to pray. Did God hear his prayers? Did God care?

Barbara and Max were at an evening church service, waiting for their three teenage children to join them. The children were coming in a separate car, making a short drive that they had made countless times before that night. With fear growing, these parents waited for their children to enter the church, but they never arrived because they were in a car accident that left Barbara and Max's older son and daughter dead and their younger son in critical care. A reckless teen driver had sped through a yield sign, cutting their car and the seatbelts in two. This driver was unhurt and unrepentant, never taking responsibility for the accident.*

Kristin and Meg are examples of women who lose one child and fear losing another one. Kristin's young daughter died in a car accident, and a few years later her son died from leukemia. Meg lost her first child to cystic fibrosis and then endured the loss of her second child to the same disease.

Wouldn't you be scared—downright terrified—in any of these situations? Job was terrified after he experienced so much loss: "That is why I am full of fear before him, and the more I think, the greater grows my dread of him. God has made my heart sink" (Job 23:15–16a TJB). Fear is defined as anxious concern and the awareness of danger. We legitimately fear the dangers in our world. Tragedy and suffering surround us. Death is inevitable for all. We fear more for the health and safety of our loved ones than for ourselves. We lay awake at night, anxious to hear our teenager's key turn the lock in the door and know that he or she has safely returned home.

We also fear circumstances, as Mary Ann knows, that are beyond our control. Susan fears unemployment for her husband, losing their home, and facing financial ruin. They have been through bankruptcy once before. Lorraine fears living alone after her husband's death to heart disease. Marcia's father left her mother during the midlife years, so Marcia fears that her husband will have an affair and leave her. Rachel fears that her abusive husband will ignore her restraining order and harm her or her children.

---

* Note: You can read Barbara and Max Garwood's complete story in my book, *An Early Journey Home*, Discovery House Publishers, 2000, pp. 163–74.

If we want to find reasons to be afraid, we can find plenty. We live with the realization that life as we know it can be turned upside down in a moment and then go horribly wrong. When my son developed strange symptoms a few years ago, I took him to see his pediatrician. His nurse called later and said, "We want your son to see a specialist. Now don't be alarmed, but the specialist is an oncologist." Of course, the nurse told me not to be alarmed because she knew I would be, just as God tells us not to be afraid because He knows we will be. Weeks later after multiple tests, doctors ruled out that my son had a cancerous tumor. Yet fear is no respecter of facts. What we fear most is the unknown, the "what if."

Coping with Fear

> When you find yourself or a loved one in the midst of suffering, it's almost always wise to let go of the "why" question.
>
> —Gregory Boyd

Each of us copes with fear in different ways. Some people, because of events in their past, are paralyzed by fear. They know for a fact that the worst can and does happen. Others have different coping skills.

When Amy learns of a tragedy in a friend's life, she analyzes it. Amy is an example of someone who dissects every part of an event, then logically concludes that this same tragedy cannot happen to her. She lives with the illusion that she can control all her circumstances. When a friend's sister dies in the hospital, she analyzes the incompetence of the medical staff, deciding that the death could have been prevented with proper care.

In chapter 4 you read about Christina's daughter, who came out of a routine medical surgery comatose because of the physician's error and later died after numerous prayer sessions. Christina's church community turned its back on Christina and her family, believing that they lacked faith. The members of this church coped with fear by avoiding what they perceived to be the source of their fears: Christina and her family and their supposed "lack of faith."

Lisa imagines God as a teacher. When she learns of multiple tragedies in friends' lives, she wonders what God is trying to teach them. The inference is that those who are right with God do not endure ongoing troubles or need these lessons.

Our faith does not follow formulas or come with a warranty. Scripture certainly teaches that the Holy Spirit is our guide and teacher (John 14:26), but God teaches us as a loving parent who holds His child's hand, gently guiding each of us with compassion. God is not an educator who hands out assignments and tests, evaluating us until we correctly understand the material and pass the final exam. Even good earthly teachers are not judges from afar. They intimately enter into the learning process with their students. This is how God guides us.

While many people may successfully protect themselves from fear through these coping methods, they fail at offering compassion and support to hurting people.

Wrestling with Theology

> When things went wrong in people's lives, whether it was about their physical or spiritual condition or some tragedy that happened to them, I don't recall Jesus ever looking for the hand of God in it. Instead, he had compassion on suffering people

and treated them like casualties of war. He expressed God's heart by bringing relief to people's suffering.

—Gregory Boyd

Fear, rooted in the anticipation of future events, forces us to wrestle with the theology of suffering. The theological arguments about reconciling how God can be all good and all powerful at the same time are centuries old. They are also worthless when we are gripped with terror and experience personal tragedy. Rabbi Harold Kushner wrote his well-known book, *When Bad Things Happen to Good People*, after his son died. He came to the conclusion that God is not all powerful and does have limitations.

In *Is God to Blame?* Gregory Boyd, who is a Christian pastor, states that "the belief that God is all-powerful does not mean that God exercises all power." This is a controversial, radical thought. He says that because God works supernaturally at some times does not mean that He always will act in those ways. The world is a war zone.

Boyd writes to challenge the "blueprint" theology that God orchestrates pain and suffering into our lives, which has caused double anguish for many hurting people. These theologians describe suffering as God's test in the refiner's fire, almost like it is an Olympic event. Boyd states that "for some people the assumption that God allows tragic events for a specific divine reason has understandably produced rage."

Through my reading of various texts on the topic of suffering, I personally have not found comfort or tangible daily help. I am not any more comforted by the idea that God is sometimes "hands-off" than that He purposefully creates suffering in my life. Our finite human brains want to find cause and effect relationships and other correlations. Some of us are comforted by thinking that God does not cause our suffering, but He allows it. This seems to be a matter of semantics and word play.

For us, these should not be the questions: Did God cause my suffering—or allow it? Is God all good? Is He all powerful? Scripture teaches that God is both all good and all powerful, in ways that we will not understand on this side of eternity. The more important questions for us are these: Is God trustworthy? Can I trust Him? That is not a theological debate but a personal decision, the only one that can calm our fears about the unpredictability of life.

The one principle that most Christian theologians agree on is that we must be completely focused on Jesus Christ. Hebrews 1:3 (NIV) states that Jesus is the "exact representation of his being." Jesus Christ is our unwavering picture of God. Boyd says, "All previous revelations of God were partial, but in Christ God is revealed fully." God suffered more in the body of Jesus Christ than we can ever imagine. He truly sympathizes with our weaknesses (Hebrews 4:15).

When we suffer, our immediate response should be to run into the arms of Jesus. Christ is our anchor, and if we are not secured to Him, we will perish. A better analogy is that Jesus Christ is our life jacket. If we take that vest off, we will drown. When children are hurt, they do not spend time analyzing if their parents are worthy of trust. They simply run into their arms for comfort and safety. We are God's children.

God may not remove our fear or the events that cause it. But He does promise to be with us in the midst of it. He carries us and keeps us afloat. Many of the thorns we live with are magnified by fear. Fear is often at the root of our anxiety and lack of trust in God.

Second Timothy 1:7 tells us that God does not give us a spirit of timidity but a spirit of power, love, and self-discipline. The

Greek translation of timidity is "terror." We do not have a spirit of fear because we have the Holy Spirit. This is the Spirit that teaches us, reminding us of what Jesus said (John 14:26). The Holy Spirit reminds us of the truth. When our human emotions of fear wreak havoc, we can trust that "there is no fear in love. But perfect love drives out fear, because fear has to do with punishment" (1 John 4:18a NIV). God is not punishing us. Rather, He is firmly holding us.

> For I, Yahweh, your God,
> I am holding you by the right hand;
> I tell you, "Do not be afraid,
> I will help you." (Isaiah 41:13 TJB)

Our challenge as believers is reconciling a myriad of verses in Scripture that clearly tell us not to be afraid with actual events in our lives that are truly frightening. The key to understanding lies in grasping how terrified God's people have been throughout Scripture and what God said to them about fear.

Biblical Struggles with Fear

"Then Moses summoned Joshua and in the presence of all Israel said to him,

> 'Be strong, stand firm; you are going with this people into the land Yahweh swore to their fathers he would give them; you are to give it into their possession. Yahweh himself will lead you; he will be with you; he will not fail you or desert you. Have no fear, do not be disheartened by anything.'"
>
> Deuteronomy 31:7–8 TJB

In the later chapters of the Pentateuch, Moses is a courageous biblical model. Yet that's not how his story began. Moses' confidence and trust in God came after years of relationship. In the early years of Moses' leading Israel, he wrestled often with fear.

In Exodus 2:14–15, Moses is frightened. He has killed an Egyptian who was beating a Hebrew, and he fears that Pharaoh will kill him, so he escapes to the land of Midian. When Moses faces God in the burning bush, he covers his face, afraid to look at Him (Exodus 3:6). Moses fears being God's spokesperson. He argues with God, "But, my Lord, never in my life have I been a man of eloquence, either before or since you have spoken to your servant. I am a slow speaker and not able to speak well." God assures Moses that He will help him speak and tell him what to say. Moses continues to argue, "If it please you, my Lord . . . send anyone you will!" This angers God. Moses does not trust God to speak through him. God then instructs Moses to speak to his brother, Aaron, who will be his mouthpiece (Exodus 4:10–17 TJB). In *Daring to Draw Near,* John White says, "Let no one deceive you. Moses was weak and fearful. He led Israel, not because he chose, but because God called him."

Other biblical models also struggled with fear. David was terrified when Saul went on a manhunt, determined to murder him. Daniel must have been afraid when he was thrown in the pit with hungry lions. The disciples were certainly afraid when Jesus was arrested and then crucified. Later in his life, Peter told suffering believers, "Who is going to harm you if you are eager to do good? But even if you should suffer for what is right, you are blessed. Do not fear what they fear; do not be frightened" (1 Peter 3:13–14 NIV). God often does not remove our enemies but rather protects us in the midst of them.

Paul was not a fearful man by nature, but when he first visited the Corinthians, he came "in weakness and fear, and with much trembling" (1 Corinthians 2:3 NIV). When he faced being shipwrecked, Paul was as scared as the other sailors and soldiers. Their ship ran aground, and "the stern was broken to pieces by the pounding of the surf" (Acts 27:41 NIV). An angel of God told Paul to "keep up [his] courage," explaining that he and the other men would not be lost, but the ship would be destroyed (Acts 27:22). God did not prevent the terrifying shipwreck, but He assured Paul of his safety. God usually tells His people, "Do not be afraid" before something really scary happens. He rarely says, "You don't need to be afraid." A popular saying tells us that we can't be brave unless we are scared.

Gideon: Why Didn't God Just Pick Someone Else?

Of all the biblical characters who fought fear, Gideon is my personal favorite. Read Judges 6–8 to appreciate the depth of his fear. This is an excellent example of God helping one of His more fearful children to accomplish His purposes. Our logical human response is, "Why didn't God just pick someone else?" Many of us can relate to Gideon's fear, anxiety, and constant questions and tests for God.

The Israelites are being severely oppressed by the Midianites when an angel of God appears to Gideon. He exclaims, "Yahweh is with you, valiant warrior!" As we observe Gideon in action, however, we see that this is a comical statement. Gideon is anything but a valiant warrior. God is trying to prepare him, perhaps build his confidence.

Like Moses, Gideon argues with God. He tells the angel of God, "Forgive me, my lord, but if Yahweh is with us, then why is it that all this is happening to us now?" Through His angel, God tells Gideon that He will rescue Israel and crush Midian. Gideon continues to argue, "Forgive me, my lord, but how can I deliver Israel? My clan, you must know, is the weakest in Manasseh and I am the least important in my family." Gideon is clear: God has definitely picked the wrong person for this job.

God is equally clear. Whether Gideon likes it or not, God has chosen Gideon. So Gideon starts testing God and asking for signs.

God graciously reassures him with tangible signs (Judges 6:21; 6:36–39). Gideon was already scared, but now that he knows he is face to face with God, he is terrified. God seems to say, "Gideon, calm down. Do not be afraid. You are not going to die."

Now God asks Gideon to do the unthinkable: tear down the altar to Baal that belongs to his father and replace it with one to God. Gideon is so scared of his family and the townspeople that he destroys the altar during the night. By the next morning, the townspeople are bent on killing him. Judges 7–8 record God's protection of Gideon through numerous battles and his transformation into a true valiant warrior. Israel was triumphant and enjoyed forty years of peace under Gideon, who was blessed in his old age (Judges 8:32b).

God Chooses Fearful People

Gideon's story shows us that God is tender and patient with fearful people. God chooses fearful people (fearful of circumstances, fearful of their inadequacies) because they have no choice but to trust Him. They will not try to accomplish tasks in their own strength. Gideon and Moses did not want the job.

We human parents raise each of our own children in different ways, depending on their temperaments, needs, strengths, weaknesses, and other factors. We even raise plants in different ways, based on their needs. Some need more water, some need less. Some need full sun, some need shade. God intimately knows us because He created us. He knows what we need and treats each of his children differently, especially those of us who are fearful and fragile.

The three times Gideon asks God for reassurance through a sign, He gives it to him. The first sign involves fire consuming meat and unleavened cakes. Gideon then asks for two different signs with fleeces, one wet and one dry. The first night, he's not fully convinced, so he pesters God again. God is unusually patient with Gideon.

When Gideon fears going into battle the next day, God tells him to go to the Midianites' camp that night to eavesdrop so that he will be encouraged. (The word *encourage* means to cover with courage.) Gideon overhears a Midianite soldier describing his dream to a friend in which the Israelites, under Gideon, are victorious. The next day Gideon and his men attack with horns, not weapons, and the Midianites flee (Judges 7:9–11). At every turn, God seems to know that Gideon needs extra care and encouragement.

God Understands Fear

> Fear, then, is a steppingstone to enrichment in our spiritual life. Without fear we are exposed to dangers of which we have little or no understanding. If through fear we learn reverence for God, our feet will be set on the road that leads to wisdom.
>
> —John White

Four main themes emerge in Scripture about fighting fear. God knows that His people struggle with anxiety and fear, in biblical times as well as today.

God tells us not to be afraid in battling the enemy. The Israelites fought earthly enemies. In numerous Old Testament examples, God delivered their enemies into their hands. Sometimes we allow ourselves to become confused when our emotions of fear over frightening events cause us to forget who our enemy really is. We face earthly enemies, but our one true enemy is the destroyer of our souls. God is already victorious, telling us, "Do not be afraid."

> Yahweh says this to you, "Do not be afraid, do not be daunted by this vast horde; this battle is not yours but God's." (2 Chronicles 20:15b–16a TJB)

> Joshua came up from Gilgal in person, bringing all the fighting men and all the bravest of his army with him. Yahweh said to Joshua, "Do not be afraid of these men; I have delivered them into your power; not one of them will be able to stand against you." Having marched from Gilgal throughout the night, Joshua caught them unaware. (Joshua 10:7–9 TJB)

God tells us not to fear while we sleep and are vulnerable. He will protect us. Lisa, like many women, couldn't sleep at night because she was afraid. Instead of studying her Bible in the morning, she began reading it at night before she went to bed. It calmed and reassured her of God's care so she could easily fall asleep.

God never sleeps, and He protects us while we rest:

> "In peace I lie down, and fall asleep at once, since you alone, Yahweh, make me rest secure" (Psalm 4:8 TJB).

> When you sit down, you will not be afraid,
> when you lie down, sweet will be your sleep.
> Have no fear of sudden terror
> or of assault from wicked men,
> since Yahweh will be your guarantor,
> he will keep your steps from the snare. (Proverbs 3:24–26 TJB)

When we fear for our safety, we can trust that God protects us around the clock. He goes before us to lead the way and comes behind to protect us: "Yahweh will go in front of you, and the God of Israel will be your rearguard" (Isaiah 52:12b TJB).

> The guardian of Israel
>   does not doze or sleep.
> Yahweh guards you, shades you.
>   With Yahweh at your right hand
> sun cannot strike you down by day,
>   nor moon at night.
> Yahweh guards you from harm,
>   he guards your lives,
> he guards you leaving, coming back,
>   now and for always. (Psalm 121:4–8 TJB)

> The angel of Yahweh pitches camp
>   around those who fear him; and he keeps them safe.
> How good Yahweh is—only taste and see!
> Happy the man who takes shelter in him. (Psalm 34:7–8 TJB)

God tells us that since He is with us, we have no reason to fear mortal man.

> With Yahweh on my side, I fear nothing:
>   what can man do to me?
> With Yahweh on my side, best help of all,
>   I can triumph over my enemies. (Psalm 118:6–7 TJB)

> This I know: that God is on my side.
> In God whose word I praise,
> in Yahweh, whose word I praise,
> in God I put my trust, fearing nothing;
> what can man do to me? (Psalm 56:9–11 TJB)

I, I am your consoler.
How then can you be afraid
of mortal man, of son of man,
whose fate is the fate of grass? (Isaiah 51:12 TJB)

Reconciling the Facts

> Fear is perhaps the first companion that will make its chill presence felt as God's hedge closes about your life. Discouragement and doubt walk hand in hand with fear.
>
> —Margaret Clarkson

The message of Scripture is clear: What can man do to me if God is with me?

No man can stand against God and His purposes. Yet most of us realize that man can do plenty to us here on earth and hurt the people we love.

Kathy's son was killed in a car accident by a drunk driver. When Michelle's husband intervened to help an older woman who was being robbed on the street, the thief punched her husband, who later died at the hospital from a brain hemorrhage, leaving Michelle a widow with four children. Tom and Susan's daughter was a young pastor's wife and new mother who was raped and killed by a carpet cleaning technician that she had hired to clean her carpets. While a young engaged couple, both counselors in a Christian camp ministry, was camping on a beach in Northern California, a killer who had been watching them shot them to death after they had fallen asleep. Most people know of examples of such horrors, and Christians are certainly not immune from tragedy.

We don't know which thought is scarier, that God is not watching (though He promises to always be with us) or that God is watching but not intervening (though He promises to protect us). Again, we wrestle with theological semantics when we should be running into the arms of Jesus.

Our world will be shaken. Yet God tells us not to be afraid when our world falls apart (Psalm 46:1–2). He tells us not to fear when we receive bad news, when police officers approach our door, or a doctor gives us a grim report.

> With constant heart, and confidence in Yahweh,
> he need never fear bad news.
> Steadfast in heart he overcomes his fears:
> in the end he will triumph over his enemies.
>
> Psalm 112:7–8 TJB

The key to living with legitimate fear, while understanding God's protection, lies in the phrase "in the end." In the end, God ultimately triumphs over our enemies. In the end, God ultimately keeps us safe for eternity. We can be confident that God will be victorious in the end.

Scripture does not say, "Do not be sick; do not be lonely; or do not be grief-stricken. But Scripture says often, "Do not be afraid." It is not enough to simply be unafraid. We must replace the emotion of fear with another one. We can only effectively get rid of one bad habit if we replace it with a constructive one. God says that keeping our minds focused on Him is the antidote to fear.

> Do not be afraid of them. Keep your minds on the Lord, who is great and to be feared . . .
>
> (Nehemiah 4:8 TJB)

> Do not be afraid; be glad, rejoice, for Yahweh has done great things. (Joel 2:21 TJB)

Focusing on God, consciously being thankful for His ultimate care and protection, is our best weapon to fight fear. Look only into the face of Jesus. Put on the life jacket.

Following God Today

> There are two things that are always the will of God and always dangerous in a fallen world: telling the truth and loving needy people. In fact, if my life of following Jesus doesn't feel dangerous, I should probably pause and check to see if it's Jesus I am following.
>
> —Gary Haugen

Following God despite our fears can be as terrifying today as it was in biblical times. Christian workers travel to dangerous locations in our world to rescue victims from torture, slavery, violence, sexual exploitation and trafficking, and other abuses. These workers put themselves in harm's way to protect the oppressed. Gary Haugen, president of International Justice Mission, says that "loving needy people as God calls us to do is not safe. It is uncomfortable, messy, difficult, and scary."

Remember: You can't be brave if you're not scared. Elizabeth Musser says, "Courage is fear that's said its prayers."

Food for Thought

- Read the familiar Psalm 23, focusing on verse 4 (NIV):

  Even though I walk through the valley of the shadow of death,
  I will fear no evil, for you are with me;
  your rod and your staff,
  they comfort me.

Some translations say, "I fear no harm." The rod was the shepherd's tool that pulled the sheep through difficult obstacles, such as crevices. The staff was used to beat off enemies, such as wolves. God guides you with His rod and protects you with His staff.

- Read Judges 7:1–4. God tells Gideon to decrease his people, lest they boast that they were victorious in their own strength. Verse 3 states, "Whoever is afraid and trembling, let him return and depart." Would you have departed or remained?

- Read Luke 21:25–28. Will you faint from fear or lift your head when Christ returns?

- Read Isaiah 7:1–4 (NIV). The Israelites learn that their enemy is advancing. Their "hearts . . . were shaken, as the trees of the forest are shaken by the wind." Does your heart shake upon learning that an event you fear may be near? God tells the Israelites, "Be careful, keep calm and don't be afraid. Do not lose heart . . ." This is God's message for you.

- Read and meditate on Psalm 91, God's psalm of protection. God says that He will lift us beyond danger (v. 14b NEB). Which verses did you find most comforting? When you wrestle with fear, practice focusing your mind completely on God.

While many people today wonder why "bad things happen to good people," the New Testament teaches that "good people" should expect to suffer (John 16:33; 1 Thessalonians 3:4). The world is, after all, a war zone.

—Gregory Boyd

Between human beings there may be no silence as loud as the silence of death.

—Barbara Brown Taylor

In order to realize the worth of the anchor, we need to feel the stress of the storm.

—Corrie ten Boom

We have this hope as an anchor for the soul, firm and secure. It enters the inner sanctuary behind the curtain.

—Hebrews 6:19b

God deflects our attempts at control by withdrawing into silence, knowing that nothing gets to us like the failure of our speech. When we run out of words, then and perhaps only then can God be God.

—Barbara Brown Taylor

7 when God SEEMS silent

Is the moment of most profound silence the
moment of God's most profound presence?
—Barbara Brown Taylor

Imagine that thieves have attacked your home and business twice in the past week, stealing most everything you own and murdering your employees. The few resources and employees that survived the attack have burned in a fire. All your employees are now dead.

You return home to learn that your house has been destroyed by a hurricane, killing all your children. You have always faithfully followed God and believed in His care and protection, so you are despairing and confused. Where is God? When you pray, He is silent. Then you become deathly sick with a painful disease. Your skin oozes with infection. When you try to rest and sleep, you have horrifying nightmares. You want to curl up and die.

Your spouse, who is angry and sick with grief, lashes out at you. Two drowning people cannot save each other. Now imagine your three closest friends and name them.

In the beginning they are supportive, but soon they say cruel things, blaming you for this tragedy. They attack you personally, critique your life, and tell you that God must be punishing you for your failures. Other times, they tell you to "cheer up" and "expect a miracle."

When you cry out to God in anguish, your friends confront you, "How dare you speak to God like that!" They believe that your words are more evidence of your sin. Your friends would rather discuss and defend their own theology than share your pain. They tell you that "God is venting His anger at you." They don't think that this tragedy could happen to them.

Everyone you know, from siblings to acquaintances, ignores you. Your closest friends are disgusted with you. While you were once respected and admired, you have now become a joke. You feel completely alone. Worse yet, you feel abandoned by God.

Now imagine, in the midst of your intense grief and pain, that you do not turn away from God. Instead, you state:

> I know that my Redeemer lives,
> and that in the end he will stand upon the earth.
> And after my skin has been destroyed,
> yet in my flesh I will see God. (Job 19:25–26 NIV)

Undeserving Job

> The book of Job should nail a coffin lid over the idea that every time we suffer it's because God is punishing us or trying to tell us something.
>
> Nobody deserved suffering less than Job and yet few have suffered more.
>
> —Philip Yancey

Job's life has been called the ultimate example of unfairness. The Bible tells us in the first verse of the book that Job is upright and blameless. Job did not deserve this catastrophe. As a result, he lived with every thorn that man experiences: despair, loneliness, illness, exhaustion, a broken heart, fear, and overwhelming loss. He felt utterly abandoned by God. When God removed the hedge of protection surrounding Job, He put everything in Satan's hands, except Job's life (Job 1:12).

When Job cannot find God anywhere—not in the east, north, south, or west (Job 23:8–9)—he realizes the one thing that matters most: "But he knows the way that I take" (Job 23:10a NIV). Though we may not be able to see God, He knows exactly where we are. Though we can't feel God's arms around us, He has not left us.

God has been present and listening to Job. In the end, God does not address Job's questions and complaints but basically asks, "Would you like to try running the universe?" Like Job, we do not see the big picture, the eternal plan. Job answers, "Surely I spoke of things I did not understand" (Job 42:3 NIV). As Peter Kreeft says, we are not led to the answer but the Answerer.

Job felt that God did not understand his suffering and would never experience it himself. Through New Testament glasses, we realize that God chose to experience that intense suffering through Jesus Christ, as He wore His own crown of thorns. "For we do not have a high priest who is unable to sympathize with our weaknesses, but we have one who has been tempted in every way, just as we are—yet was without sin" (Hebrews 4:15 NIV). Jesus, our great high priest, knows our suffering and pain because He experienced it himself.

God the Creator asks us—through Job—if we would like to try running the universe. The complexities are beyond our comprehension, analogous to explaining calculus to a preschooler. He tells us that He has experienced every pain that we suffer. Hebrews 5:7 states that during His days on earth, Christ offered up prayers and petitions with loud cries and tears to the one who could save Him from death. Like Job, even Christ cried out to His Father God and felt completely abandoned before His death.

> In the silence surrounding his death, Jesus became the best possible companion for those whose prayers are not answered, who would give anything just to hear God call them by name. Him too. He wanted that too, and he did not get it. What he got, instead, was a fathomless silence in which to cry out.
>
> —Barbara Brown Taylor

When God Doesn't Answer

> I cry out to you, O God, but you do not answer.
>
> Job 30:20a NIV

The silence of God is mentioned several times in Scripture, so it must have a constructive purpose. In our human relationships, the deeper the relationship is, the more comfortable is the silence. God may seem silent at times, but perhaps we are not listening on the right frequency or receiving the answer we want to hear.

We often misinterpret God's call to wait and be patient as His silence. Waiting, being patient, and persevering were much better understood in biblical times than they are today. We live in a culture where people expect to have their needs and wants immediately met. Unsolved problems are unacceptable.

The word *patient* is derived from the Latin word *patiens,* which means to suffer or endure. Gordon Smith says that "true courage is characterized by patience—patience with God, whose work is often imperceptible and slow."

Similar to Job, Jeremiah suffered from multiple thorns and sometimes felt abandoned by God. In Lamentations 3:25–26 (TJB), he states:

> Yahweh is good to those who trust him,
> to the soul that searches for him.
> It is good to wait in silence
> for Yahweh to save.

You might imagine that you are in the waiting room of life. You do not understand God's silence. You may feel like an accident victim sitting in the emergency room, waiting hours to see a physician. When will the nurse call your name? But that is not how God works. You were taken directly to surgery, and you are now in recovery. Though you feel like you are endlessly waiting, you are slowly healing on God's timetable.

When Nehemiah arrived in Jerusalem to begin his campaign to start rebuilding the wall, he waited three days before inspecting it. Jesus asked His Father three times to spare Him from death, and silence was the only response. Three days passed between Christ's crucifixion and His resurrection. Waiting from three days to hundreds of years, God usually does not act immediately. Scripture tells us that we are living in the last days before Christ's return. Believers have been waiting for two thousand years.

The disciples often did not understand why Jesus refused to take immediate action when a need arose. My favorite examples of this occurred in boats on the sea. When the disciples were struggling at the oars because of storms and severe winds, Jesus waited to give help. We are quick to remember that Jesus calmed the storms, but more important is the fact that He waited. The disciples' boat almost capsized in one storm while Jesus slept (Mark 4:35–41). Jesus prayed on the mountain and was alone on the shore during another storm. He waited until the fourth watch before walking on the water to calm the wind. He watched his men struggle for hours (Mark 6:45–52).

As His good friends mourned, Jesus did not even rush to help Lazarus. Mary and Martha had sent for Jesus when Lazarus was sick, but He waited two days before traveling. Lazarus had been in the tomb for four days when Jesus arrived. We understand now that Jesus waited to perform His miracle of raising Lazarus from the dead, just as He waits to perform bigger miracles in our lives today. These miracles originate in His silence as we wait. The most significant miracle is that we trust Him in the storm.

> Brothers, as an example of patience in the face of suffering, take the prophets who spoke in the name of the Lord. As you know, we consider blessed those who have persevered. You have heard of Job's perseverance and have seen what the Lord finally brought about. The Lord is full of compassion and mercy. (James 5:10–11 NIV)

Food for Thought

- Have you experienced God's silence? Have you misinterpreted it as abandonment by God?
- In James 5:10–11, we read about what the Lord *finally* brought about, suggesting a concept similar to the one in verses stating "in the end." When God is slow to act, do you assume that He is inactive? Ponder how absurd it is that we unconsciously give God deadlines.
- Psalm 40:1 (NIV) states, "I waited patiently for the Lord; he turned to me and heard my cry." Think about how our culture, even Christian culture, does not understand the disciplines of waiting, patience, or perseverance.

> A simple rule of thumb: God only leads us one step at a time.
>
> —Gordon Smith

Sorrow is not a stranger to any of us, though only a few have learned that it is not our enemy either.

—John and Stasi Eldredge

When we surrender them to God, the tragedies that threaten to destroy or blight our lives become the source of our deepest understanding.

—Henry Gariepy

In the darkness of the tunnel merely "keeping on" becomes a miracle.

—Verdell Davis, whose pastor husband
and three friends died in a plane crash
while returning from a Focus on the Family
men's retreat

8 when there is NO MIRACLE: living with permanent loss

Faith in God offers no insurance against tragedy.
—Philip Yancey

Sometimes there is no earthly miracle on this side of eternity. We live with the thorn of permanent loss. Our loved one dies. Our divorce is final. Our body deteriorates with disease. Life is forever changed. No matter the length and intensity of our prayer vigils, God does not perform the miracle that we long for.

God may have restored Job's resources and family in the end, but any grieving parent will tell you that having another child does not replace the deceased one. Job lost ten children.

Christians are not insulated from tragedy and multiple losses. After parents have experienced the death of their child, their marriages are often strained and can end in divorce, as tragedy follows tragedy. After Rebecca's young daughter died from leukemia, her husband left her and filed for divorce. Rebecca told me that the death of her daughter was easier to cope with than her husband's abandonment because "his corpse was still walking around."

Sometimes the possibility of a miracle is more painful than accepting that no miracle will occur. We know that God can intervene in any situation. John and Karen's teenage son struggled with learning disabilities and addictions. As committed Christians and devoted parents, they did everything they could to help him, seeking assistance from counselors and doctors and placing him in a rehabilitation facility. Their son seemed to be recovering. Friends, family, and church members continued to pray. Yet months later, John and Karen's son accidentally overdosed and died.

> Save me, O God;
> for the waters have risen up to my neck.
> I sink in muddy depths and have no foothold;
> I am swept into deep water, and the flood carries me away.
> I am wearied with crying out, my throat is sore,
> my eyes grow dim as I wait for God to help me.
> Psalm 69:1–3 NEB

Stolen Miracles

We feel sometimes that we have been robbed of a miracle. In 2006, while thirteen miners in Sago, West Virginia, were trapped beneath the ground, their families went to church to pray. As they were praying, they received word from mining company executives that their loved ones were still alive. The miners' survival was a sheer miracle. God had answered the prayers of the relatives. But three hours later, the family members were told that the information was incorrect. In fact, only one miner was still alive. One relative said, "They took away our miracle."

In 2006, a teenage boy went to his school in Joplin, Missouri, with an assault rifle, terrorizing students and administrators, but his gun jammed when he began firing. No one was hurt. Was it a miracle? No such miracle occurred in 2006 in an Amish schoolhouse in Nickel Mines, Pennsylvania; at a mall in Omaha, Nebraska in 2007; at Columbine High School near Denver in 1999; or at Virginia Tech in 2007. Even churches are no longer immune from these shootings. In a now-infamous December 2007 incident, a gunman who had developed a grudge against a Christian missionary training center shot two young people at the training center outside of Denver and travelled to a Colorado Springs church hours later, where he shot and injured a father and killed his two daughters as they were leaving the church. After a church security guard shot and wounded the gunman, the gunman killed himself.

Jack, an accomplished teenager with a strong faith in Jesus Christ, was in a car accident that left him paralyzed. His faith was evident to family, friends, and members of various churches who helped with his care. He died two years after the accident. He did not live as Joni Eareckson Tada has. Joni became a quadriplegic in 1967 as the result of a diving accident; she now has a Christian ministry that serves the disabled community and has written over thirty-five books. She is well known and respected for her service to the Christian community. For every Joni, there are thousands of injured individuals who do not live to have phenomenal ministries and experience the opportunity to witness worldwide through their suffering.

I have known a few individuals who experienced physical healing, but for every one of those cases, I know of hundreds with the same solid faith in God who were not healed. I was forced to face this fact when I worked as a therapist in a children's hospital. Even more challenging is the realization that sometimes one family's miracle can be another family's tragedy. Mark was nearing death as he waited for a kidney transplant. His survival seemed hopeless. Diane's twenty-five-year-old son, Randy, was killed in an auto accident. Randy's kidney saved Mark's life. Mark's parents, wife, and children celebrated the organ donation as a miracle. While Mark's family was shedding tears of joy, Diane's family was shedding tears of sorrow.

A Thin Veil

> Now we see only puzzling reflections in a mirror, but then we shall see face to face. My knowledge now is partial; then it will be whole, like God's knowledge of me.
>
> 1 Corinthians 13:12 NEB

During the time I worked with terminally ill children in the hospital, I also knew several people in my personal world who lost children. I felt bombarded by pain and loss, and as a person in her twenties without much life experience, my faith was shaken to the core. I could not understand God's silence. There is no loss as devastating as the parent's loss of a child, a grief that no one fully recovers from. I realized that either my God was inadequate and powerless, or my view of God was inadequate. Yet if we trust God only when He makes sense to us, that is not faith. We have faith in that which is unseen and not understood. I learned that it was my knowledge of God that was inadequate. Someday I will fully know Him, just as He fully knows me, but that will not occur here on earth.

I began to grasp how thin the veil is between here and eternity. I saw that my finite view of God was not only distorted but also untrue. When countless parents prayed for their children to be healed, God permanently healed them, never to be sick or hurting again. They were safe with Him. One grieving mom explained to me:

> When our young daughter was diagnosed with cancer, I knew that God could heal her and would heal her. I never doubted Him for one minute. As the year of hospitalizations and treat-

ments passed, she grew worse, but I remained confident that God was waiting to reveal His great power in our hour of greatest weakness. Our church and friends continued to pray for the miracle. Then my precious daughter began to suffer. I surrendered completely to God, fully realizing that we cannot understand His ways. One day I prayed, "God, I do not understand. Please heal her or take her home and make her whole with you." My daughter peacefully died during the night.

When we pray for our spouses, children, parents, siblings, and friends to be healed, God will heal them, but we are unable to see through the veil. We may pray for temporary healing here on earth, and sometimes He grants it—but sometimes God permanently heals them by taking them to be with Him.

The Same Faith

Hebrews 11 describes two types of suffering. In Hebrews 11:32–35, sufferers such as David and Gideon experience miracles here on earth. They escape death, are victorious in battle, see the mouths of lions closed and raging fire quenched, and receive God's promises. Yet the sufferers in Hebrews 11:35–40 are destitute, tortured, imprisoned, scourged, sawn in two, killed by the sword, and experience other atrocities. These sufferers have the same faith in the same God as the first group. Hebrews 11:32–35 describes men who are spared from suffering and delivered *from* tribulation. This has been called "Noah faith." Hebrews 11:35–40 describes men who are delivered *through* tribulation. This has been called "Job faith."

God promises that we will be saved and delivered, sometimes from suffering and sometimes through suffering. We do not get to choose. We will probably experience both types of deliverance throughout our lives. Each of us will experience permanent healing at the close of our days here on earth, on a date that we will not choose either.

God also promises that evil will not harm us (1 John 5:18). Pain and evil are very different. Tremendous pain may envelop us, but we are protected from evil. Human beings aspire to live a life without pain, but that is not a biblical goal.

> Even though I walk through the valley of the shadow
> of death,
> I will fear no evil, for you are with me (Psalm 23:4
> NIV).

> The Lord will guard you against all evil; he will guard
> you, body and soul.
> The Lord will guard your going and your coming, now
> and forevermore (Psalm 121:7–8 NEB).

Left Behind

> Our light and momentary troubles are achieving for us an eternal glory that far outweighs them all. So we fix our eyes not on what is seen, but on what is unseen. For what is seen is temporary, but what is unseen is eternal.
>
> 2 Corinthians 4:17–18 NIV

Temporary healing—or permanent healing? Saved from tribulation—or through tribulation? Does God cause—or allow—pain? Do these thoughts truly comfort us when we are in the midst of deep grief? We may have peace that our loved ones are safe, but that doesn't take away our pain of being left behind. Annette knows what it is like to live with the thorn of multiple permanent losses.

Annette grew up in a loving Christian home. Her parents were dedicated to serving Christ in their church, their family, and their work. Annette told me, "I remember as a child being thankful that my family had not suffered any profound tragedies, but I think that I also had a sense that because we were such a good Christian family this was probably God's reward for our devoted service to Him."

Annette attended a Christian college where she met her future husband, whose parents had been career missionaries. Annette and Jon married, confident in God's faithful care of them and their families.

A few years later, Annette's younger sister, Kristi, was in a car accident on her way home from college for Christmas break. Through the Christmas season and the weeks to come, their family lived at the hospital by Kristi's bedside. Kristi died of complications from her internal injuries in mid-January, 1990. Annette explains her journey:

> I couldn't believe that God would do this to our family—that He would punish us in this way. My reaction was despair, hopelessness, and anger at a God who would treat one of His most faithful families like this. Rather than drawing close to Him, finding comfort in His love and trusting that He works all things for our good, I sought ways of bringing comfort to myself. There seemed to be no meaning in this tragedy, and I became bitter as I looked at the vast numbers of people around me whom God allowed to live. It made no sense that He would take this beautiful, talented girl who had wanted to serve Him with her musical talent and leave drug addicts and sexually immoral young people without motivation or goals who weren't following Christ.
>
> One year later, Jon and I were expecting our first child. We named her Kathleen Kristi Lynn, after my sister. Her birth didn't take away the thorn of my sister's death, but it did ease the pain. I focused on caring for my newborn baby. Two years later, in 1993, our son was born. I swept all of my anger and bitterness toward God under the carpet, where I could easily ignore it, redirecting my focus to caring for my family.
>
> In December the following year, we endured another heartbreaking Christmas. My 35-year-old husband was diagnosed with acute leukemia. The initial tests indicated a 60-percent chance of recovery. Should I hope that my hus-

band would recover, or was God going to torment me once again? I wanted to be home caring for my young children, but instead I spent my time with Jon at the hospital during his chemotherapy and follow-up treatments. I couldn't understand why God was doing this to our family.

Jon seemed to be responding well to treatment in the first six months after his diagnosis. The doctors declared that he was in remission. Seven months after diagnosis, though, he relapsed and needed a bone marrow transplant. Despite the transplant and the doctors' best efforts, Jon died, leaving me a 35-year-old widow with two toddlers to raise. I marveled at the cruelty of a God who would allow me to hope for a miracle and then pull the rug out from under me again.

The losses seemed to multiply. I was incredibly lonely and increasingly bitter and angry. I needed to find a full-time job to support us and endured financial hardships. I struggled with depression. All I had wanted was to be a work-at-home wife and mother. Why would God deny me this? Why were my children being forced to grow up without a father?

Today I still don't have answers to these "whys." I did not find the way out of this forest of thorns by myself. I was led out by the Holy Spirit, who came to me in my brokenness and bitterness, reminding me that God is good, that He delights in preserving His people who are suffering, but usually not in the ways we want or expect. I began to see God's hand. Though my children were left fatherless, God gave me loving parents who moved nearby to help us. God provided me with a fulfilling job. And, most recently, He has given me a godly husband who fathers my children with a love and tenderness that could only be God-given.

I now realize that God never owed me anything. In spite of my anger and ingratitude, He has shown mercy and kindness, providing for all our family's needs. I can trust Him. Like

Paul at the end of his life, after multiple disappointments, I can say, "But the Lord stood by me and strengthened me … The Lord will rescue me from every evil deed and bring me safely into his heavenly kingdom" (2 Timothy 4:17–18).

Annette does not hide her pain and grief. Old Testament grievers did not hide their pain. They rent their clothes, displaying their grief to the world. As they recovered, they repaired the ripped seams and wore their clothes inside out. They continued to mourn. The scars of loss remain for a lifetime.

> For I am convinced that neither death nor life, neither angels nor demons, neither the present nor the future, nor any powers, neither height nor depth, nor anything else in all creation, will be able to separate us from the love of God that is in Christ Jesus our Lord.
>
> Romans 8:38–39 NIV

Food for Thought

- What life circumstances have resulted in your "ripped seams"? What "scars" do you have that have been caused by loss?
- Think about times in your life when you were delivered from tribulation and times when you were delivered through tribulation.
- Read Psalm 77, which I call the Griever's Psalm. May God's words comfort you.

> Blessed are those who mourn, for they will be comforted.
>
> Matthew 5:4 NIV

Only after a personal tragedy do we come to grips with the problem, because it is our personal problem—as though what happened to other humans was not our problem. To live thoughtfully with Christlike love we must allow ourselves to be disturbed by the grotesque realities surrounding us and sympathetically enter into the nightmarish suffering of others. Tragedy strikes people every day.

—Gregory Boyd

The heart of the wise is in the house of mourning,
the heart of fools in the house of gaiety.

Ecclesiastes 7:4 TJB

Part 2 Entering the Pain Clinic

While we need not assume there is a divine purpose leading to our suffering, we can and must trust that there is a divine purpose that follows from it. Hence our suffering is not meaningless.

—Gregory Boyd

But although Christians suffer, and thus experience the same pain that others encounter, there is a difference: we suffer with hope.

Gordon T. Smith

It is His purpose to bring us through the waters, not to have us be lost in their depths.

Margaret Clarkson

We live in God with our circumstances rather than living in our circumstances with God.

Mark Labberton

offense vs. DEFENSE: survival tools 9

Christ is seldom a reality unless He is first a necessity.

—anonymous

In part 1, you may have identified with those feelings of despair, loneliness, weariness, fear, and grief that most of us experience at some point in our lives. Perhaps you have lived with struggles similar to the ones described by contributors. Hopefully you are comforted to know that you are not alone. Your experience of living with thorns is perhaps more common than you thought. The goal of part 2 is to equip you with survival tools for that journey, tools that God has already given us. It is my hope that these are tangible ways that will help you run into your Father's arms.

These survival tools are based on scriptural truth, embodying a God-given approach to life that can help us live on the offense instead of the defense. Living on the defense is already a weak position. We want to be prepared and proactive, not reactive, to challenging circumstances. Victim mentality may be comfortable at times, but it is ultimately destructive. Some people find their identity in being victims of tough circumstances. Instead, we want to be hopeful people who completely trust in God, not defeated, resigned people who have given up.

We must also understand that these steps are not a magic formula to transform our situation. Following God is not a cause/effect negotiation. We face life, knowing that God is all powerful and can intervene to change our circumstances. We also know how much God loves us and that nothing touches us that is not filtered through His loving hands. If we must endure painful situations for a week, months, years, or a lifetime, we are confident that God is working a different type of miracle in our lives. If we are human beings who live on this earth, we know that often one type of thorn is removed from our lives, only to be replaced by another. Sometimes our thorns multiply.

Just as patients who live with chronic pain find help in pain management clinics, we can also learn ways to manage our pain, whether it is physical, emotional, mental, or relational pain. We will probably never be pain-free, but we can live significant, purposeful lives as followers of Jesus Christ.

As I have read Scripture through the years, I have observed how our biblical models faced tough times and what tools they used to cope. I have also had the opportunity to interview numerous people who have faced similar difficult times. The same methods have worked in their lives today. One of my favorite seminary professors, Dennis Guernsey, suggested to one class that we shut the theological treatises and simply ask godly people how they have survived life's challenges. For Professor Guernsey, this wasn't a theoretical exercise. A few years later, he died of a cancerous brain tumor. His own toughest challenge was yet to come.

My hope is that part 2 of this book marries scriptural methods with current real-life experience and application. God's ways are always effective, regardless of time, place, or situation. The first two steps are our foundation for the ones to follow in later chapters. The terms *survival tools* and *steps* are used interchangeably because a tool is only effective if we take action and use it. May this process comfort you as you grapple with your thorns. May God "transform [your] valley of troubles into a door of hope."

> But I will court her again and bring her into the wilderness, and speak to her tenderly there. There I will give back her vineyards to her and transform her Valley of Troubles into a Door of Hope.
>
> Hosea 2:14–15a, *The Living Bible*

Entering the Pain Clinic

> To suffer in God's way means changing for the better and leaves no regrets, but to suffer as the world knows suffering brings death.
>
> 2 Corinthians 7:10 TJB

Survival step #1 is to mourn and seek God. A consistent pattern in the Old Testament emerges when God's followers face extended painful circumstances. The books of Nehemiah and Daniel reveal excellent examples. In chapter 1, Nehemiah asks Hanani and his men about the Jews and Jerusalem: "'Those who escaped from captivity,' they replied, 'who are back there in the province, are in great trouble and humiliation: the walls of Jerusalem are in ruins and its gates burned down.' On hearing this I sank down and wept; for several days I mourned, fasting and praying before the God of heaven" (Nehemiah 1:3–4 TJB).

When Nehemiah learned of the devastation in Jerusalem, he was distraught and brokenhearted. He sank down and wept. He mourned not for a few hours, but for several days. He fasted and prayed before God. He begged God to hear him (Nehemiah 1:11). Compare this with Daniel's experience:

> In the first year of his reign I, Daniel, was perusing the scriptures, counting over the number of years—as revealed by Yahweh to the prophet Jeremiah—that were to pass before the successive devastations of Jerusalem would come to an end, namely seventy years. I turned my face to the Lord God begging for time to pray and to plead with fasting, sackcloth and ashes. I pleaded with Yahweh my God and made this confession . . ." (Daniel 9:2–4 TJB)

Seventy years? That may seem a long time to endure successive devastation, but God's people sometimes suffered for hundreds of years through generations. Daniel mourned with sackcloth and ashes. He prayed and pleaded with God. He confessed his sins and the sins of his people in the verses that follow. Like Nehemiah, Daniel also begged God to hear him (Daniel 1:18–19).

Nehemiah, Daniel, and other prophets mourned their unchanged circumstances and grieved for God's people. They wept, prayed, fasted, confessed their brokenness, and pleaded with God to hear them. Today we may not wear sackcloth and ashes, but we can embrace the same pattern of mourning and seeking God. We also have confidence through Jesus Christ, our advocate, that God hears every word.

> Grieve, mourn and wail. Change your laughter to mourning and your joy to gloom. Humble yourselves before the Lord, and he will lift you up.
>
> James 4:9–10 NIV

Survival step #2 is to trust that God will restore us. In the midst of mourning broken relationships, chronic illness, exhaustion, isolation, depression, permanent loss, or other pain, we can trust that God will rebuild among the thorns. These are the miracles that we don't expect. Even when we human beings rebuild after fires or earthquakes, we create dwellings that are better, stronger, and more beautiful than the original buildings. Imagine what God can do: "And the nations left around you will know that I, Yahweh, have rebuilt what was destroyed and replanted what was ruined. I, Yahweh, have spoken, and I will do it" (Ezekiel 36:36 TJB).

God is in the restoration business. He restored us to himself in Jesus Christ. He also daily reconstructs our lives on the ruins of devastation.

> Yes, Yahweh says this: Your wound is incurable, your injury past healing.
> There is no one to care for your sore, no medicine to make you well again.
> All your lovers have forgotten you, they look for you no more.
>
> Jeremiah 30:12–14a TJB

You probably have scars from the thorns you have lived with. You may feel that the wounds in your life will never heal, and they keep being reopened. You may feel abandoned by all your lovers. Yet one lover, Jesus Christ, your bridegroom, will never abandon you. God assures us at the end of Jeremiah chapter 30: "But I will restore you to health and heal your wounds—it is Yahweh who speaks" (Jeremiah 30:17a TJB).

Restoration

> You shall be called Rebuilder of broken walls, Restorer of houses in ruins.
>
> Isaiah 58:12b NEB

Restoration is sometimes confused with erasure. God restores our lives. He does not erase them. When God restored us to Himself, He forgave our past sins, but He did not remove them from our memory. Forgiving is different from forgetting. Remembering our past sins only makes our salvation more powerful. We know what we have been saved from.

Similar to restoring a damaged antique piece of furniture or a historic home, this process of rebuilding our lives can be a labor of love. When God rebuilds our lives, our past pain does not instantly disappear, as though it were erased. Kathleen, who died after her ninetieth birthday, knew the miracle of restoration.

Kathleen's childhood was chaos. When Kathleen was six years old, her mentally ill mother was placed in a mental institution, and Kathleen never saw her mother again. She was left to be raised by an alcoholic father with a volatile temper who neglected her. They lived in poverty in a boarding house. Half-siblings, from her mother's first marriage, resented Kathleen. Her half-brother raped her when she was a young child. She didn't understand what he was doing, but she knew that it was bad.

Kathleen married her high school sweetheart and was truly happy for the first time in her life, but he died in an accident a year after they married. Later she remarried and found herself in a miserable marriage. Her husband was distant and self-consumed. She desperately wanted children, but they were unable to have any. In mid-life, she found Jesus Christ through attending Bible

Study Fellowship. She enjoyed the new experience of having close friends in a Christian community. She discovered that God was miraculously transforming her from the inside out. She was then able to lovingly nurse her father, and later her husband, to their deaths.

In the last decades of her life, Kathleen developed a debilitating degenerative muscle condition. She became weaker as she aged and was finally unable to move. Confined to her bed or wheelchair in medical facilities, Kathleen continued to pray for her friends and hospital workers. Though she had not been able to have biological children, she had countless spiritual children and grandchildren. Many families from the churches she attended had embraced Kathleen and adopted her into their lives. They visited her, advocated for her, and cared for her until her last day on earth. She died from pneumonia. Kathleen often told people, "If God could change me, in all my brokenness, He can change anyone." She felt that she was a living testimony to God's miraculous power. She also believed that God gave her back all the love that she had been denied as a child.

Kathleen lived with multiple thorns during her ninety years. She was a living example of Isaiah 58:12. God rebuilt her broken walls and restored her life from ruins.

> Then I will make up to you for the years
> that the swarming locust has eaten.
>
> Joel 2:25a, *New American Standard Bible*

Pain Clinic

- Think about a difficult situation, past or present, which you grieved, seeking God with your whole heart. Did you weep, fast, pray, or beg God to hear you?

- Think about a time in your life when you experienced devastation and ruin.

  Did God rebuild your life in new, unexpected ways? How? Ponder this theme of restoration that runs through Scripture, realizing that restoration is not erasure.

- Think about the current thorns in your life. Have you lived with them for weeks, months, or years? Now think about past thorns in your life. Did God change your circumstances or change you? Did He bring about a different kind of miracle that you never would have chosen or planned?

- Read Acts 15:16–18. God rebuilds from the ruins. We often read the Old Testament through New Testament eyes. We also need to read the New Testament through Old Testament eyes. God's plans for ultimate restoration are beyond what we can imagine.

> When our souls lie barren in a winter which seems hopeless and endless, God has not abandoned us. His work goes on. He asks our acceptance of the painful process and our trust that He will indeed give resurrection life.
>
> —Elisabeth Elliot

A man in sorrow is in general much nearer God than a man in joy. Gladness may make a man forget his thanksgiving: misery drives him to prayer.

—George MacDonald

When Scripture and your experience clash, do not run away from the tension. Let it become the energizer of earnest prayer. In the Christian life you need *more* tension, not less, if you are to do the will of God.

—John White

Prayer can be hard, and apparently unanswered prayer can require discipline we may not readily have. Prayer may require us to face our theological doubts and longings. Prayer may cause us to face intractable evil. Prayer will lead us to times when we don't understand God or his ways. This is all part of identifying with the God who shares our burdens and carries our sorrows.

—Mark Labberton

Honesty with God 10

I cry aloud to the Lord;
    to the Lord I plead aloud for mercy.
I pour out my complaint before him
    and tell over my troubles in his presence.
When my spirit is faint within me
    thou art there to watch over my steps.

Psalm 142:1–3a NEB

I recently learned about a remote monastery where the monks rise early in the morning to pray through all 150 psalms daily. The book of Psalms has been called the heart of the Bible. This is significant for those of us who live with thorns, because the

Psalms are our most powerful model for communicating with God. They embody authentic prayer, rooted in honesty. We can see why this community of monks starts their day by immersing themselves in the psalms to focus on their relationship with God.

Prayer without complete honesty—without being naked before God—is empty. The psalmists knew that. David knew that. Job knew that. God's most intimate followers have known that for centuries.

We know that too in our own relationships. Our closest relationships are those in which we feel the most secure; they are safe places where we can be completely honest. We know that we are unconditionally accepted and loved. We have also experienced relationships that are strained. We are guarded and careful about what we say. One wrong word or glance can undo our best efforts. We can never relax.

Honesty is interwoven with healthy intimacy. Imagine that your children or spouse go through the motions of having a relationship with you but are never completely honest. They hold something back. It would break your heart. God does not want to have a strained, guarded relationship with us. He longs for us to be open and transparent with Him. God's arms should be the safest place we run to when we are struggling.

Worse than having a guarded relationship is giving or receiving the silent treatment when we are angry with one another. We cut off all communication. God grieves when we give Him the silent treatment and shut Him out. He can certainly handle our pain and anger and longs to be in relationship with us.

Job trusted God enough to be completely honest with Him. In Job 7:11 (NIV), he tells God: "Therefore I will not keep silent; I will speak out in the anguish of my spirit, I will complain in the bitterness of my soul." How have we believers come to think that complaining to God is unbiblical? God never condemned Job for expressing his deepest thoughts and emotions, though He did condemn Job's friends for judging and attacking Job. Job's friends seemed more comfortable talking about God than talking to Him.

Our next survival step is critical for surviving our thorns. ***Survival step #3*** is to have an honest, vital, ongoing conversation with our Father, holding nothing back. This is authentic prayer. A formulaic prayer life will not cut it. Sanitized, structured prayers, devoid of true emotion and struggle, are meaningless.

Are you usually this honest with God?

> But I am here, calling for your help,
> praying to you every morning:
> why do you reject me?
> Why do you hide your face from me?
>
> Wretched, slowly dying since my youth,
> I bore your terrors—now I am exhausted;
> your anger overwhelmed me,
> you destroyed me with your terrors
> which, like a flood, were around me, all day long,
> all together closing in on me.
> You have turned my friends and neighbors against me,
> now darkness is my one companion left. (Psalm 88:13–18 TJB)

This is "on-your-knees," anguished prayer. Psalm 88 (TJB) begins, "Yahweh my God, I call for help all day, I weep to you all night." Verses 8 and 9 continue: "In prison and unable to escape, my eyes are worn out with suffering." Psalm 88 ends with verses 13–18. This psalm is unusual because it does not follow the pattern of most lament psalms. There is not one shred of hope or affirmation of God's care. Yet this psalm is here in Scripture for us to pray through. We are moved by its raw honesty.

> Another form of tainted trust is dishonesty with Jesus. Sometimes we harbor an unexpressed suspicion that he cannot handle all that goes on in our minds and hearts.
>
> —Brennan Manning

Pouring Out Your Heart to God

> The psalms function not only as discipline and instruction about how to pray but also as an invitation and authorization to speak imaginatively beyond these words themselves.
>
> —Water Brueggemann

Most lament psalms, those in which God's people pour out their pain, follow a consistent pattern. The psalmist begins with pain and hopelessness, then moves on to affirm the truth about God and who He is (praise). Finally the psalmist declares his trust in God and desire to follow Him. Trusting God depends on our understanding of who He truly is. Read Psalms 31, 42, and 77 in their entirety as examples of this pattern.

Psalm 77 (TJB) moves from despair to declaring truth:

v. 1 Loudly I cry to God,
loudly to God who hears me.
[Are you listening, God?]

vv. 2–3 When in trouble I sought the Lord,

all night long I stretched out my hands,
my soul refusing to be consoled.
I thought of God and sighed,
I pondered and my spirit failed me.

vv. 11–12 Remembering Yahweh's achievements,
Remembering your marvels in the past,
I reflect on all that you did,
I ponder on all your achievements.

v. 13 God, your ways are holy!
What god so great as God?

Psalm 31 (TJB) moves from grief and sorrow to trust:

vv. 9–10 Take pity on me, Yahweh,
I am in trouble now.
Grief wastes away my eye,
my throat, my inmost parts.

For my life is worn out with sorrow,
my years with sighs;
my strength yields under misery,
my bones are wasting away.

v. 14 But I put my trust in you, Yahweh,
I say, "You are my God."

Psalm 42 (TJB) moves from despair and oppression to hope and praise:

v. 3 I have no food but tears,
day and night;
and all day long men say to me,
"Where is your God?"

vv. 10–11 Nearly breaking my bones
my oppressors insult me,

as all day long they ask me,
"Where is your God?"

Why so downcast, my soul,
why do you sigh within me?
Put your hope in God: I shall praise him yet,
my savior, my God.

There are about fifty lament psalms, and they comprise the largest group, occurring much more frequently than praise, creation, wisdom, or liturgical psalms. God's people are wrestling with Him, pouring out their troubles and frustration. Lament psalms are a response to heartache in real life crises.

People in trouble came to the temple to plead with God. Note in 1 Samuel 1:13–15 that Hannah is so upset when she comes to the temple that Eli, the priest, assumes she is drunk. She answers him, "No, my lord . . . I am a woman in great trouble; I have taken neither wine nor strong drink—I was pouring out my soul before Yahweh" (v. 15 TJB). God's people worshiped Him with intimate honesty. David, as well as others, wrote psalms out of despair. The community shared their pain.

Walter Brueggemann, in *The Psalms and the Life of Faith*, states, "Laments show clearly that biblical faith, as it faces life fully, is uncompromisingly and unembarrassedly dialogic." We are in a passionate conversation with God. Brueggemann also says that the lament psalms follow the stages of classic grief work: denial, anger, bargaining, depression, finally leading to acceptance. He calls them "distress to relief" psalms, from "self to God." Human beings will always struggle with unwanted change and multiple types of losses as we cry out to God.

Brueggemann points out that the lament psalms have been purged from the life of the church, which "attests to the alienation between the Bible and the church." Said another way, the lament psalms are often ignored because they are too brutally honest for most churches and believers to grapple with.

When I was a new believer in college decades ago, I learned a formulaic method for prayer based on the letters *ACTS*: Adoration, Confession, Thanksgiving, and Supplication. The prayer moved from praising God, through confession and giving thanks, to petitioning Him. The biblical model God gives us in the lament psalms is radically different, even the opposite of ACTS. First we pour out all our pain to God, pleading with Him to rescue us. Then we move to praising and trusting Him, remembering who He is and knowing that He hears us. Formulas are never relational. Conversations with God are powerful exchanges.

Survival step #3 is our foundation for living with thorns. We must live our days in honest communication with our Lord. When we are too distraught to pray, we can pray through the psalms. The lament psalms are especially comforting. They can be a springboard for our own conversations with God.

No Secrets

> I will tell you my most terrible secret. I get very mad at God sometimes, especially when he lets me get hurt . . . This is a pretty well-kept secret, especially among evangelicals and fundamentalists.
>
> —Peter Kreeft

Keeping secrets is destructive in any relationship. Throughout Scripture, God's people did not hide their anger and disappointment with God as a terrible secret. They shared their pain, hurt, anger, and frustration with a listening God. At times, they even argued with Him. The best example is Jonah.

When God does not destroy Nineveh, Jonah "[falls] into a rage" (4:1 TJB). He is furious with God and has no tolerance for His ways, especially for God's compassion for the people of Nineveh. Jonah thinks these people are worthless. You can bet that Jonah is yelling at God. He says twice in chapter 4 that he "might as well be dead as go on living" (vv. 3, 8 TJB). God confronts Jonah, "Are you right to be angry?" Jonah replies, "I have every right to be angry to the point of death" (v. 9). Many of us know the end of the story. God makes his point with Jonah using a visual aid, the castor-oil plant, but only after Jonah has had a full-fledged tantrum. God demonstrates the selfishness of Jonah's attitude: "You are only upset about a castor-oil plant . . . Am I not to feel sorry for Nineveh . . . in which there are more than a hundred and twenty thousand people who cannot tell their right hand from their left?" (vv. 10–11 TJB).

If you become angry with God sometimes, you are not alone. You may keep this secret from other Christians, but you cannot hide your anger from God.

God's Honesty with Us

Now we come to the more challenging part of being honest with God. Good and healthy relationships and conversations are two-sided. God wants us to be honest with Him, but He also wants to be honest with us. ***Survival step #4*** is accepting that honest exchange, which is difficult for many Christians. It requires reading Scripture in its entirety, not just limiting ourselves to the parts of Scripture that are comfortable for or accessible to us. Can you imagine reading any other book this way? If we read a novel this way, we would never understand the plot. If we read a textbook this way, we would never grasp the material. The Bible is both a phenomenal story and a life textbook.

God felt so strongly about being completely honest with us that He put His words into a permanent record, the Scriptures, and so we must engage in Scripture immersion, reading the Bible in its entirety. This task requires hard work. We need to understand the whole of Scripture—not disjointed parts—viewing every passage in the context of its chapter, book, and the entire story. The pick-and-choose smorgasbord approach to Scripture, reading passages that are comfortable or familiar, may be uplifting and encouraging on a daily basis but will not lead to long-term maturity. We must move from milk to solid food, from being comfortable to being challenged. Our goal is to know God as fully as we can, just as He wants to know us. This is the key to understanding our thorns, lest we think that God has forgotten us or made a mistake in our lives.

Gregory Boyd encourages us always to view God through the lens of Jesus Christ. Jesus is God incarnate, the full reflection of His father. We must read the Old Testament through New Testament eyes as well as the New Testament through Old Testament eyes.

I guarantee you that if you practice Scripture immersion, you will read parts of the Bible that will make you uncomfortable and some passages will downright upset you. In *Daring to Draw Near*, John White writes:

> If we close our minds to everything about God that makes us uncomfortable, we are going through empty motions when we pray. We pray to a god we have ourselves fashioned for our comfort and not to God as he is. True prayer is to respond to the true God as he reveals more of himself by his Spirit in his Word. Prayer defined in such terms can be a terrifying experience.

Several parts of Scripture unsettle me, including passages that deal with mass murder, the treatment of concubines, torture, rape, frequent killings, the stoning of Stephen, the beheading of John, and more, but the passage that upsets me most is Judges 11:29–40. Read Judges 11, noting that Jephthah, son of Gilead, was a valiant warrior. Jephthah was also the son of a harlot and was driven away by his half-brothers, who told him, "You have no share in our father's inheritance." Apparently his father did nothing to stop them, and Jephthah fled. His life was filled with rejection and heartache.

When the Ammonites attacked Israel, the elders of Gilead went to Jephthah to ask him to be their commander. Of course he replied, "Was it not you who hated me and drove me out of my father's house? Why come to me when you are in trouble?" (v. 7 TJB). Jephthah finally agreed to help them. "The spirit of the Lord came on Jephthah" (v. 29 NIV), so we understand that God was with him. Jephthah made a vow: "If you give the Ammonites into my hands, whatever comes out of the door of my house to meet me when I return in triumph from the Ammonites will be the Lord's, and I will sacrifice it as a burnt offering" (11:31–32 NIV). The Lord delivered the Ammonites into the hands of the Israelites. It was a severe defeat.

When Jephthah returned home, his daughter, his only child, came out of the house to meet him, dancing and playing the tambourine, probably overjoyed to greet her father. Jephthah was heartbroken (v. 35), yet he kept his vow. He sacrificed his only child to God. Scholars speculate that Jephthah foolishly made a rash vow, ignorant of God's commands prohibiting human sacrifice. Yet God tests Abraham by asking him to sacrifice his only son. Jephthah is grief stricken to follow through on his vow, incorrectly believing that he is honoring God.

In Genesis 22, God spared Isaac's life and Abraham's grief. An angel of the Lord stopped the sacrifice, saying, "Do not harm him, for now I know you fear God. You have not refused me your son, your only son" (vv. 12–13). Why did God intervene to spare Isaac's life but not the life of Jephthah's daughter? These were their only children. Though I have heard Genesis 22 read often in church, I have never heard Judges 11 discussed.

Then I remember that God sacrificed His only Son to rescue us.

We must look at the entirety of Scripture.

Pain Clinic

- Read Psalm 142, thinking about how pouring out your troubles to God leads to trusting Him. Practice being completely honest with God.

- Practice Scripture immersion, seeking God's honesty with you. Begin by praying through one psalm a day.

- Consider finding a program that best fits your lifestyle that will help you read through the entire Bible in one year. Numerous programs and organized study Bibles are available.

> But how shall I speak of the glories I have since discovered in the Bible? For years I have read it with an ever-broadening sense of joy and inspiration; and I love it as I love no other book. Still there is much in the Bible against which every instinct of my being rebels, so much that I regret the necessity which has compelled me to read it through from beginning to end.
>
> —Helen Keller

God hears all poured out agony, but he longs to be something more than a celestial pacifier. He wants people in their suffering to come to him. For he is himself the gift we really need.

—John White

Traditional churches and seeker churches alike have made an art form of figuring out how to make unchurched people feel comfortable. The best intention of most churches is to show people the comfort of God's love in Christ. However, it ought to be of more than passing significance that comfort has not been high on God's methodology list. Wilderness? Exodus? Exile? Incarnation? Crucifixion? Taking up your cross? These elements of the biblical narrative suggest that God does not prize comfort.

—Mark Labberton

To attribute all difficulty to the evil one is to give evil more credit than is due. In so doing we easily fail to embrace difficulty as a cross through which God is bringing grace to bear in our lives and in the lives of others.

—Gordon T. Smith

11 Aligning our Vision with God's Vision

The Lord confides his purposes to those
who fear him,
and his covenant is theirs to know.
My eyes are ever on the Lord,
who alone can free my feet from the net.
Psalm 25:14–15 NEB

When you are immersed in Scripture, clearly hearing God's honesty through His Word, you will experience a challenging but miraculous change in your life. You will begin to see your unchanged circumstances through God's eyes. You will begin the hard work of aligning your vision with God's vision, embracing it as a painful privilege.

Psalm 25:14 in *The Jerusalem Bible* states, "The close secret of Yahweh belongs to them who fear him." Psalm 25:14 in the *New English Bible* states, "The Lord confides his purposes to those who fear him." This is the language of intimacy. Imagine the people you confide in, those you trust to know your intimate secrets. Keeping secrets from loved ones is unhealthy. Sharing with them evidences your mutual trust and a strong relationship. God longs to have an intimate relationship with you in which He shares His secrets. He confides in you about His purpose through His Word. Do your purpose in life and God's ultimate purpose line up, or are they directly opposed?

If you feel entangled by your thorns, aligning your vision with God's vision is the best way to "free your feet from the net."

Thy Will Be Done

> I learned long ago that God's purpose in redeeming us is not to primarily make our lives happy, healthy, or free from trouble. God's purpose in redeeming us is to make us more like Jesus.
>
> —Joni Eareckson Tada

Marcie is concerned about her women's prayer group at her church. They meet weekly to discuss their needs (often wants) and bring them to God in prayer. She says that those needs sound like a Santa Claus list.

Imagine that whenever you visit your mom and dad, you spend your time together asking them for things. Parents laugh when their children call from college only when they need money. They're just happy to hear from them. Relationships based on expressing and fulfilling needs are immature. God wants us to be in a mature relationship with Him.

Jesus taught us to pray the Lord's Prayer, another example of how we should communicate with God:

> Our Father in heaven,
> thy name be hallowed;
> thy kingdom come,
> thy will be done,
> on earth as in heaven. (Matthew 6:9–10 NEB)

Jesus instructs us to pray for our needs (not our wants) when He tells us to say, "Give us this day our daily bread," and our prayer for our needs should follow our prayer for God's will to be done. First we pray for God's will to be done. John is more specific: "We can approach God with confidence for this reason: if we make requests which accord with his will he listens to us; and if we know that our requests are heard, we know also that the things we ask for are ours" (1 John 5:14–15 NEB).

God hears us and answers our requests when we make them in accordance with His will. You may have heard people praying who end their prayers with the phrase, "But your will, not ours, be done, Lord," and this comes across as an afterthought. Ending our prayers by asking for God's will to be done is backwards. There is no "but" involved. We must start with that phrase, not end with it. First we pray for God's will to be done on earth and in our lives, and that common vision is what shapes our communication with God. We seek to know through Scripture what God's purposes and secrets are.This understanding protects us from the tyranny of self-absorption. Practicing it will revolutionize your prayer life.

> "Instead, you ought to say, 'If it is the Lord's will, we will live and do this or that.'"
>
> James 4:15 NIV

Sharing God's vision requires aligning our desire and purposes with God's desire and purposes. First, God wants a deep, intimate relationship with His children. Then He wants us to become Christlike. As our Father, He is raising us, and His goal is for us to mature and become more like Jesus. This is a lifetime learning process.

> And we know that in all things God works for the good of those who love him, who have been called according to his purpose. For those God foreknew he also predestined to be conformed to the likeness of his Son, that he might be the firstborn among many brothers.
>
> Romans 8:28–29

When experiencing a difficult situation, people often quote Romans 8:28: "In all things God works for the good of those who love him." Just as important is the fact that we have been called according to His purpose, and that purpose is that we will become like Christ. "Good" does not mean comfortable or happy. It refers to being conformed to Christ's image. Romans 8:26–27 are critical preceding verses, explaining that the Spirit prays for us because we do not know how to pray. The "Spirit intercedes for the saints in accordance with God's will" (8:27b NIV).

Philippians 2:5 and 1 Peter 4:1 encourage us to have the same attitude (mind) as Christ. We are to be imitators of God (Ephesians 5:1) and live for His will (1 Peter 4:2). Ephesians 4:13 calls us to become mature, attaining the full measure of perfection found in Christ. How do we become more like the Suffering Servant if we have never suffered? Rarely does someone exhibit the gift of mercy and compassion that has not experienced some suffering. We cannot feel someone else's pain if we cannot feel our own.

In *The Dangerous Act of Worship*, Mark Labberton says that we share the universal need to be turned inside out and right side up. Scripture bears out that God does not prize comfort. Labberton describes this "spiritual transformation as our deepest and most profound human need." He explains: "This transformation is the most difficult thing in the world. Why else would it require the death of God's only Son? It is the highest price for the most costly and difficult change. So when we talk about spiritual transformation—being remade into the image of Jesus Christ—let's remember that it is profound and costly, that it required death for there to be life."

Can we have our lives spiritually overhauled without facing any challenges? Can we develop the Christlike qualities listed in Galatians 5 and 2 Peter 1 of love, joy, peace, patience, kindness, goodness, faithfulness, gentleness, self-control, perseverance, and godliness without our character being chiseled? These fruits of the Spirit are evidence that we reflect Jesus Christ, and they are qualities intended for all believers. It shouldn't surprise us that these characteristics are honed through practice and training. We are being molded into Christ's image.

God does not raise spoiled brats. Hebrews 12 explains that God disciplines us because He loves us. Imagine that you, an earthly parent, gave your children everything they wanted exactly when they wanted it. Imagine that you never required them to wait for anything or work to earn the things they want. You often gave them what they wanted even when it was harmful (for example, junk food) because you were so tired of hearing them whine and complain. You never denied them any desire or expected them to put someone else's needs above their own. If this were all true of your child rearing, you would not be happy with the results. In your efforts to make your children happy in the moment, they would not mature into healthy adults. In fact, they would be miserable and make everyone around them miserable. Your children would be spoiled, unable to function in the real world that expects them to behave responsibly, putting others before themselves.

Even as earthly, imperfect parents, we shudder at the thought of a child who has never been told no. Yet God is a perfect parent. He does not make mistakes in raising His children. He will do what is best for us for the long run. His vision extends through eternity.

Prosperity Message

> And we rejoice in the hope of the glory of God. Not only so, but we also rejoice in our sufferings, because we know that suffering produces perseverance; perseverance, character; and character, hope.
>
> Romans 5:2–4 NIV

The image of a God who says "no" or "wait" is an unpopular concept. God often says "no" or "wait for eternity" to His children. We live in an age of entitlement, where this biblical message directly clashes with our culture. The media programs us for immediate gratification. Our generation is saturated with the message that we should have what we want when we want it; otherwise, we are deprived. Rampant credit card debt attests to the severity of this problem. Baby boomer parents who wanted to give their children as perfect a life as possible, with every imaginable opportunity, are now realizing that what may have appeared to be "deprivation" could have been life's best teaching tools.

Tragically, this philosophy has seeped into parts of the church. The prosperity gospel is popular again and attracting the masses. It rears its head every few decades. The prosperity gospel preaches that God wants us to be happy, experiencing success in all areas of life (finances, health, and relationships). It seems to teach that God wants us to have heaven on earth now. This health-and-wealth gospel is not rooted in the entirety of Scripture. It is sprinkled with Scripture, not saturated in it. We are called as believers to enter into Christ's suffering, to share the pain of others, not avoid it. God calls us to lay down our lives—not elevate them—to seek the well-being of others before our own. A theology based on avoiding pain doesn't wash. Suffering should not surprise us: "Dear friends, do not be surprised at the painful trial you are suffering, as though something strange were happening to you. But rejoice that you participate in the sufferings of Christ, so that you may be overjoyed when his glory is revealed" (1 Peter 4:12–13 NIV).

Intending to be fair to proponents of the prosperity message, I read a popular best-selling book on this topic by a well-known author and pastor. I found one chapter on enduring hardship toward the end of the book, yet the author's message—that suffering was designed to make a person stronger and more successful in the end—remained consistent to the end of the book. Living with permanent suffering was not a consideration.

Job's life of prosperity was demolished, yet Job was blameless (Job 1:1; 2:10). Job's friend, Elihu, told him that God "pays a man according to his work and sees that he gets what his conduct deserves" (Job 34:11 NEB). Elihu also said this about men who turn to God: "If they listen to him, they spend their days in prosperity and their years in comfort" (Job 36:11 NEB).

In Job 42:7, God told Job's friends that they were completely wrong. The only reason that their lives were spared was that God asked Job to pray for his friends, and God heard Job's prayers. The book of Job should put to rest any notion that God rewards those who follow him with a prosperous life.

The ancient Roman poet Horace said, "Adversity reveals genius. Prosperity conceals it." A more relevant version of this famous quote for us would be, "Adversity reveals your true relationship with God. Prosperity conceals it."

Approaching Eternity

> Rejoice in that day and leap for joy, because great is your reward in heaven.
>
> Luke 6:23 NIV

In contrast to pursuing heaven on earth, biblical truth teaches that our ultimate goal is spending eternity with God. This is the epitome of delayed gratification. In Luke 6:23, Jesus is speaking to His disciples. "That day" He refers to is not a day of joy in heaven but the ones on earth that bring suffering. (Read Luke 6:17–26.)

Before Jesus was betrayed, He explained to His disciples that He would soon be leaving. Peter asked the Lord where He was going.

"Jesus replied, 'Where I am going, you cannot follow now, but you will follow later.'"

Peter's response was, "Lord, why can't I follow you now?" (John 13:36–37 NIV). In different ways, we ask the same question: "Why can't we be with you now, Lord? Why can't we taste heaven now?"

He answers, "Not now. Later." Jesus further explains:

> Do not let your hearts be troubled. Trust in God; trust also in me. In my Father's house are many rooms; if it were not so, I would have told you. I am going there to prepare a place for you. And if I go and prepare a place for you, I will come back and take you to be with me that you also may be where I am. You know the way to the place where I am going (John 14:1–4 NIV).

Someday we will hear the words that Jesus spoke to the criminal who was executed with Him: I tell you the truth, today you will be with me in paradise (Luke 23:43).

There is a thin veil between our life on earth and eternity, but we cannot see through it. God promises that we will be pain-free, completely whole people, experiencing never-ending, unimaginable joy on the other side of eternity. If we could view our lives today backwards—from the vantage point of eternity—it may not diminish our earthly pain, but it will enlarge our vision.

Meg lost two children to cystic fibrosis. While most of us will be leaving our children behind when we die, Meg will be greeted by her children, who are waiting for her in heaven. Can you imagine their reunion? Eternity will be the complete flip side of our pain on earth.

Survival step #5 is to align our vision with God's vision, understanding His goals, so that we have an intimate relationship with Him, become mature and Christlike, and lift our eyes toward heaven.

> The people there pleaded with Paul not to go up to Jerusalem. Then Paul answered, "Why are you weeping and breaking my heart? I am ready not only to be bound, but also to die in Jerusalem for the name of the Lord Jesus." When he would not be dissuaded, we gave up and said, "The Lord's will be done."
>
> Acts 21:12–14 NIV

Pain Clinic

- Read Ephesians 1, focusing on verses 9–11. Think about the mystery and purpose of God's will.

- Does your vision align with God's vision? Are your goals the same as His?

- Read James 4, reviewing verse 15 in context: "Instead, you ought to say, 'If it is the Lord's will, we will live and do this or that.' As it is, you boast and brag. All such boasting is evil" (NIV). Also, note James 4:3, which addresses asking God for wants versus needs: When you ask, you do not receive, because you ask with wrong motives, that you may spend what you get on your pleasures (NIV).

- Recite the Lord's Prayer, remembering the important preface in Matthew 6:8: God knows what our needs are before we ask Him.

> Don't ever think that God is on your side.
> Pray earnestly that you are on God's side.
>
> Abraham Lincoln

The hardest part of relationships is being in them.

—Nicole Johnson

What is your pain? It is the experience of not receiving what you most need. It is a place of emptiness where you feel sharply the absence of the love you most desire. To go back to that place is hard because you are confronted there with your wounds as well as with your powerlessness to heal yourself.

—Henri Nouwen

understanding OUR FAMILY'S thorns

> Your future depends on how you decide to remember your past.
>
> —Henri Nouwen

We are halfway through our treatment sessions at the pain clinic. This is a good time to review the first five survival steps before looking at how we can cope with our family's thorns.

Survival Step #1	Mourn and seek God.
Survival Step #2	Trust that God will rebuild your life.

Survival Step #3	Engage in honest communication with God, pouring out your heart.
Survival Step #4	Be open to God's honesty with you, immersing yourself in the entirety of Scripture.
Survival Step #5	Align your visions and goals with God's vision and goals.

Whatever thorns you live with are probably entangled with your family's thorns. Perhaps you feel that your pain was caused by your parents' or grandparents' struggles. Some of you may have had an intact, happy childhood but now live with your spouse's thorns and family line's problems. Others of you may live with the most painful type of family thorns, those experienced by your children.

Therapists tell us that we cannot begin to heal from pain until we are aware of its source and clearly understand it. This complete understanding requires very hard work, sometimes years of work. It is not an intellectual understanding but an understanding of the heart, one that changes us at our core.

Survival step #6 is to understand your family's thorns. You cannot change the way you live with your family's thorns until you face them head on and honestly grapple with the truth.

Living with Our Family's Thorns

> The more a daughter knows the details of her mother's life—without flinching or whining—the stronger the daughter.
>
> —Anita Diamant

Anita Diamant's quote rings true as I reflect on my own life. My mother, Maria, is a remarkable grief survivor. When Maria was five years old, her mother died from a sudden illness. A few years later, her older brother died after an accident. Lost in his grief over his wife's and son's deaths, Maria's father became distant and abusive; he coped with his pain in destructive ways. Maria's childhood best friend died as a young woman, while she was giving birth. During her ninety years, Maria has also survived the loss of two husbands, a younger brother who was murdered, and numerous close friends. She told me once, "I learned at an early age that when I loved someone, that person was taken from me." My mother is an exceptionally strong, intelligent, and passionate woman who has always exemplified survival skills for me in the face of life's challenges. Her thorns have only strengthened me.

Later I would marry a man whose family had also suffered much grief. When my husband was thirteen years old, his father and only sibling died in an accident. My husband was unable to deal with his grief until later in life, during his forties, which is common for children who lose parents. Our family's thorns are laced with grief on both sides.

Stacey's adult daughter, Corrine, suffers from mental illness. She has been diagnosed with schizophrenia and bipolar disorder. Corrine has trouble holding jobs and does not have health insurance. Sometimes she sees a doctor and takes her needed medication, but often she doesn't. Since Corrine is an adult, Stacey cannot force her to be hospitalized or receive medical care. She has considered having Corrine live with her but realizes that her behavior is unpredictable. Stacey and her husband (Corrine's stepfather) would feel unsafe. Stacey could never confidently leave Corrine alone in their home.

Julia was raised by alcoholic parents. She didn't realize they were alcoholics until she reached her twenties. She thought that her parents were gregarious, liked to party, and drank a bit too much. She knew they had been through bankruptcy. Julia knew that she had to work to put herself through college because her parents couldn't help. She finally grasped the severity of their addiction:

> Through helping a struggling friend one day, I read the list of characteristics of adult children of alcoholics, and I was shocked to discover that I had every one. I had recently become a Christian and was beginning the slow process of forgiving my alcoholic parents. I naively thought that God would change them. Through prayer and God's miraculous healing, I knew that "we" [God and I] could fix them (a prominent belief of children of addicts). Recovery for children of alcoholics requires realizing that we can't fix anything.
>
> My mom was neglectful but never cruel. It was easier to forgive her than my dad. He was a self-seeking man who always put himself first. Forgiveness is not blind. I visited my parents on a regular basis, but I never left my children in their care or allowed them to drive my children anywhere. I knew they mixed driving and drinking. I didn't allow my parents to drink when they visited my home.
>
> My parents are now deceased. They were alcoholics until they died. I forgave both of them and had a relationship with them. When my mom fell, I took care of her in my home as she recovered. She fell often due to her drinking. I made many trips to the emergency room with her. After my dad died, I paid my mom's expenses because she was financially destitute.

Julia set clear boundaries to protect her sanity and the safety of her family. She courageously forgave her parents in tangible ways and compassionately loved them through their brokenness. While alcoholism can often continue through generations, Julia's four children witnessed the devastation that addiction causes and have vowed never to use alcohol.

Tessa and her brother were raised and abused by a mother who was addicted to prescription drugs and suffered with manic depression. Sometimes they hid in a neighbor's yard, unknown to the neighbor, to escape their mother's rages and being beaten with a belt. Other times, their mother went to bed for days, neglecting their care. As a teenager, Tessa would go home at lunch to make sure that her mother had not overdosed. Tessa's father was unable to confront his wife and made excuses for her. He tried his best to take care of his children when he was home from work.

The most complicating factor was that Tessa's parents were pillars of their church, active and committed believers. Her dad was a deacon; her mother led Bible studies. They hid their family secret from everyone, appearing to be the perfect Christian family. The ritual of constantly attending church activities was another one of Tessa's mother's addictions. In addition to the abuse, Tessa grew up with a distorted view of God and faith. God was part of the lie. Tessa told me, "If God was our parent, I wanted no part of that. It would have been far better for me if my mom had not wrapped up Christianity with her illness."

As a teenager and young adult, Tessa sought out comfort in destructive relationships with men. At her lowest point, she contemplated suicide. Through an extended process of therapy, healing, and forgiving her parents, Tessa fully recovered. Today she has a healthy relationship with God and is a loving mother to her own children. She is an active philanthropist, helping children who cannot help themselves.

> Don't talk, don't trust, don't feel is supposed to be the unwritten law of families that for one reason or another have gone out of whack.
>
> —Frederick Buechner

The Biblical View of Family Thorns

We view in Scripture two truths about family thorns to be held in tension. The first truth is that we are not isolated. God sees us in the context of our family line. The most well-known verse on this topic is Numbers 14:18–19 (TJB): "Yahweh is slow to anger and rich in graciousness, forgiving faults and transgression, and yet letting nothing go unchecked, punishing the father's fault in the sons to the third and fourth generation.

Here is a more severe example of punishing a family line:

> No Ammonite or Moabite, even down to the tenth generation, shall become a member of the assembly of the Lord. They shall never become members of the assembly of the Lord, because they did not meet you with food and water on your way out of Egypt, and because they hired Balaam ... to revile you. The Lord your God refused to listen to Balaam and turned his denunciation into a blessing, because the Lord your God loved you. You shall never seek their welfare or their good all your life long. (Deuteronomy 23:3–6 NEB)

"You shall never seek their welfare" does not sound like Jesus' mandate to turn the other check. Punishing a family line to the third, fourth, or even tenth generation seems grossly unfair in our culture. I try to imagine that I will suffer for something my great-great-great grandparents did. Worse yet, I imagine my great-great-great grandchildren suffering because of mistakes I've made. Yet we have a thorough God, one who "lets nothing go unchecked." Again, we are reading parts of Scripture that make us uncomfortable, but these verses are not the whole story.

We logically understand that our lives do not exist in a vacuum. People who were abused as children by their parents often abuse their own children, and the chain continues through generations.

Chemical dependency, drug addiction, and alcoholism have been linked to genetic chemical imbalances that affect generations. The reality is that the problems of one generation do flow into the next. Without intervention, specifically the miraculous healing touch of God, these patterns will continue.

Some of the most loving, dedicated mothers I know were severely abused as children. Some of the most capable, successful people I know were raised by alcoholics. In each case, they made conscious choices to change the course of their lives. They did exactly what Caleb did in Numbers 14.

Read Numbers 14:18–19 about punishment to the third and fourth generation in the context of the entire chapter. Numbers 14:24–25 (NEB) states:

> None of those who have flouted me shall see this land. But my servant Caleb showed a different spirit: he followed me with his whole heart. Because of this, I will bring him into the land in which he has already set foot, the territory of the Amalekites and the Canaanites who dwell in the Vale, and put his descendants in possession of it.

Caleb not only changed course for himself but for his descendants. He consciously chose to follow God with his whole heart. He broke the chains of his family line's disobedience to God.

We are not imprisoned by our family's thorns. We are not ultimately responsible for our parents' and extended family's brokenness, our spouse's struggles, or our children's poor choices. Yet we are certainly responsible for our actions toward these people in our lives. We also cannot blame them or use them as an excuse for our own problems.

- Fathers may not be put to death for their sons, nor sons for father. Each is to be put to death for his own sin. (Deuteronomy 24:16 TJB)

- The man who has sinned is the one who must die; a son is not to suffer for the sins of his father, nor a father for the sins of his son. To the upright man his integrity will be credited, to the wicked his wickedness. (Ezekiel 18:20 TJB)

Each of us is called to account only for ourselves. No matter how our family line stretches out behind us or in front of us, the path is clear. God asks us to follow Him with our whole heart.

Jesus realized that His disciples incorrectly believed that struggles were a result of a family's sin:

> As he went along, he saw a man blind from birth. His disciples asked him, "Rabbi, who sinned, this man or his parents, that he was born blind?"
> "Neither this man nor his parents sinned," said Jesus, "but this happened so that the work of God might be displayed in his life. As long as it is day, we must do the work of him who sent me" (John 9:1–4a NIV).

Jesus healed this blind man, restoring his sight. Jesus brings a new understanding that is radically different from views held by Old Testament believers, ideas that were quite foreign to His disciples. Jesus teaches that our earthly problems are not caused by our sin or the sin of our families. Instead, our struggles can be grand opportunities for God to transform our lives and display His miraculous power.

Reality Check

You may sometimes think that your life would be radically different if you had enjoyed an ideal childhood. You may wonder if your marriage would be easier if your spouse had not endured childhood problems. If you are a normal, caring parent, you are probably concerned about the impact your struggles have on your own children. You understand the critical role that family relationships play in the development of any human being.

We receive cultural messages that our goal is to provide as near perfect a childhood as possible for our children. Yet raising children in a bubble, isolated from struggles, has proved to be quite damaging. The Millennials (children born after 1981) are the most protected and over-monitored generation in American history. They have also been called the "Generation of Entitlement." Among the character traits associated with the Millennials is the pursuit of perfection, and psychologists have seen an increase in eating disorders, suicide attempts, chemical addictions, depression, bipolar disorder, a lack of focus and drive, narcissism, and other problems. The pressure to achieve an ideal life, young childhood through adulthood, is taking a toll.

Dr. Robert Brooks of Harvard Medical School says that mistakes are the experiences that prepare youngsters for their futures. A life shielded from mistakes and learning to overcome obstacles is an unhealthy one.

It is a serious matter that many Christian parents are following this trend with gusto, shielding their children from problems and any perceived bad influences. Children learn by watching their parents. Observing parents who follow God with their whole heart and survive problems, such as financial struggles, illness, marital stress, family conflict, tragedy, and more, is the best preparation for life. It is also the best preparation for following God, no matter what life holds. I know too many young people who have walked away from God who grew up in "ideal, problem-free" Christian homes. Maybe they never learned the need for God. I know other young people whose families trusted God and struggled with painful circumstances. Their relationship with God is rock solid. Their faith has been tested. Perhaps your faith is solid because of the example your parents set when facing difficult trials.

Living with thorns gives us a unique opportunity to teach our children about trusting God and following Him. It is not our problems that will impact our children but how we face our problems that will change their lives and prepare them for following God when they face their own thorns. Hopefully they will take the clear path, following God with their whole hearts.

> Faith is not taught but caught along the way.
>
> —Mark Schultz

Pain Clinic

- Read Ezekiel 18 about individual responsibility. Through no fault of our own, we often live with thorns resulting from the behavior of our parents, spouse, or children. Note in Ezekiel 18:10–13 that a father is not held responsible for his son's disobedience and in Ezekiel 18:14–20 that a son who does not imitate his father's misdeeds and crimes but follows God will certainly live.

- Spend some time thinking about your family members' thorns. How did they survive them? Has their example strengthened you, or caused you pain? Perhaps interviewing family members and gleaning more information would be helpful in trying to understand those challenges.

- Focusing on Caleb's example in Numbers 14:24–25, think about how following God with your whole heart frees you from being imprisoned by your family's thorns.

> There are no graduates in the school of human pain.
>
> —Margaret Clarkson

He that cannot forgive others breaks the bridge over which he must pass himself; for every man has need to be forgiven.

—Thomas Fuller

Forgiveness is the fragrance of the violet which still clings fast to the heel that crushed it.

—George Roemisch

If you cannot free people from their wrongs and see them as the needy people they are, you fasten yourself to the past and let your hate become your future.

—Lewis Smedes

Practicing Forgiveness

13

We are never so free as when we reach back into our past and forgive a person who caused us pain. We cannot erase the past; we can only heal the pain it has left behind.

—Lewis Smedes

If your wounds have been caused by another human being, then embracing forgiveness is another important step for surviving your thorns. ***Survival Step #7*** is to practice forgiveness. Note that Step #7 is not stated like this: Forgive the person who caused your thorns. That would imply a finished act. True forgiveness is a daily, ongoing process. Perhaps a parent, spouse, child, friend, or stranger has inflicted great harm on you or someone you love.

Perhaps the source of your pain continues. This is how one wife explains her journey of forgiveness:

Sometimes I envy people who have forgiven some great wrong in their past and moved on. They have forgiven people who are no longer present in their daily world. More challenging is forgiving someone you live with–a difficult spouse, rebellious teenager, or angry aging parent. When we forgive someone who causes us daily pain, we wrestle with the meat of the gospel–unconditional love–on a moment to moment basis. This is the miraculous face of true forgiveness. When my husband and I reconciled after he curtailed an affair, well-meaning friends said to me, "I would never put up with that. I could never forgive him." What if God had said that about me and walked away from the cross?

Forgiveness is a complicated process that is often misunderstood. Many people confuse the results of forgiveness with the actual process of forgiveness. Before looking at what forgiveness is, let's think about what forgiveness is not.

What Forgiveness Is Not

> When you forgive someone for hurting you, you perform spiritual surgery inside your soul . . . Detach that person from the hurt and let it go, the way a child opens his hands and lets a trapped butterfly go free.
>
> —Lewis Smedes

Forgiveness is not a feeling.

Lasting forgiveness is hard work, requiring painful honesty. Denial and forgiveness cannot coexist. We must fully acknowledge the pain we have suffered before healing can begin. Forgiveness is a tangible action. We can act in a forgiving manner when we do not feel forgiving. We stop seeking revenge. We perform an act of kindness for someone who has hurt us. "I forgave him through clenched teeth," said one betrayed wife about reconciling with her unfaithful husband. Forgiving someone is not dependent on human emotions. Obeying God transcends our feelings.

Forgiveness is not blind denial.

Forgiveness does not accept or condone the actions of the offender. Forgiveness does not tolerate abuse. It does not give the offender permission to continue hurting us or victimize others. We have a forgiving God who is also holy and just. Forgiveness does not mean remaining in an abusive marriage or allowing children to spend the night with a grandfather who is a child molester. It is not quietly enduring a spouse's affairs or addictions. Forgiveness does not allow a serial murderer or rapist to go free from prison to commit other crimes. Forgiveness does not release an offender from the consequences of his or her actions. Forgiveness is not injustice.

Forgiveness does not guarantee reconciliation.

When God forgives us, He develops an intimate relationship with us. We become His children. This is the ideal picture of forgiveness: forgiven to be reconciled. Many forgivers have experienced this miraculous circle of restoration, but others have not. A wife who fears for her safety and the safety of her children cannot reconcile with an abusive, alcoholic husband who refuses to seek treatment. Often a restraining order is in place. Sometimes we cannot reconcile with abusive parents because they are deceased.

"Forgiveness depends on me. Reconciliation depends upon us," says Lewis Smedes. Forgiveness is not a magic formula that guarantees changed lives and improved relationships. Those who reconcile with difficult spouses, parents, or children are not promised ideal relationships. They have learned to draw clear lines between challenging relationships and abusive ones.

Forgiveness does not make sense.

Forgiveness is not logical or fair. It doesn't make sense to the world, sometimes even to fellow Christians in the church. The word *forgiveness* is derived from the word *gift.* We offer gifts with no strings attached or expectations of the receiver. Forgiveness can often meet with resistance from those around us. It is a courageous act.

Forgiveness is not forgetting.

The most misunderstood concept of forgiveness is that it involves forgetting. "I don't think I could ever forget. Otherwise I could not remember the miracle of forgiveness," explains the daughter of an alcoholic mother who beat her daily. The miracle of forgiveness requires remembering first. It then moves to conscious forgetting or choosing not to remember.

> I will forgive their wickedness, and will remember their sins no more. (Jeremiah 31:34 NIV)

> I will forgive their iniquity and never call their sin to mind. (Jeremiah 31:34 TJB)

Often this verse is incorrectly quoted: "I will forgive their iniquity and forget their sins." There is a subtle, but critical, difference between "forgetting" and "not remembering." God never forgets sin, or He would not have sacrificed His precious son, Jesus, to rescue us. We would be lost, without hope, if God truly had forgotten our brokenness and sinfulness. When we become His children through Jesus Christ, God chooses not to remember our sin. He does not call it to mind.

> Our ability to forgive is in direct proportion to our genuine identity with Christ. Our reluctance to forgive reflects the distance in our relationship with Christ.
>
> —Chuck Lynch

One Forgiver's Journey

Larry describes his journey of forgiveness:

I grew up without a father. My mother had different partners, and on the weekends different dads would come to pick up my siblings for visitation. I longed to have a dad, but no one ever came for me. I searched for my biological father for years and finally found him through tracing county records. I didn't want anything from him but to stand face to face and hear him acknowledge that I was his son.

I had to take care of myself and learned to be independent at an early age. I've worked in the construction trade to earn a living since I was a teenager, and today I own a successful business. I married and had children. After years of effort, the day finally arrived to approach my dad.

I waited in my truck outside his house until he came out. I walked up to my dad, and it was like looking in a mirror. He knew exactly who I was. We were identical in appearance; I was the younger version. He was not pleased to see me. "What do you want?" he demanded. "Do you want money? Your mother was a whore . . . I doubt I'm your real father." He said cruel things as I tried to explain that I only wanted to meet him.

My mother may not have been perfect, but she always loved me and took care of me the best she could. My lifelong quest to hear my father acknowledge me, much less apologize for abandoning me, was hopeless. I walked away from him, never to contact him again.

I think the Bible is pretty clear. Its command may be painful, but it's not complicated. If we don't forgive others, our Father God will not forgive us. I may not have an earthly father who gives one rip about me, but I do have an eternal Father who loves me, takes care of me, and will never leave me or abandon me. I forgive the dad who failed me. It's not a choice. I obey my true Father who saved me.

What Forgiveness Is

> Unforgiveness is the bind that ties—chokes and contorts, poisons and paralyzes. Forgiveness releases, straightens, and energizes. Forgiveness is a willingness to bear the pain. When we choose to forgive, we meet the pain head on.
>
> —Jane Rubietta

Forgiveness is a process.

Forgiveness is a process, not a single event. Forgiveness is a daily choice and a lifelong journey. It takes time to heal. Often the more grievous the offense, the more time is required to practice forgiveness.

Philip Yancey states, "Forgiveness must be taught and practiced, as one would practice any difficult craft." Christians are called to become experts at forgiveness, mirrors of Jesus Christ. It does not happen overnight. When our pain resurfaces through the years, we realize that we have more to forgive. After Corrie ten Boom had forgiven the SS officer who assaulted her in the Nazi concentration camp and was responsible for her sister's death, she sought the advice of her pastor, because hideous memories kept returning. He pointed to the church bell. He explained that even after the rope of the bell was no longer pulled, the sound continued for some time. Painful memories wind down like the church bell.

Practicing forgiveness spills over into all our other relationships. We are to have a continual attitude of forgiveness, prepared to forgive future offenses when they arise. Forgiveness looks backward and forward.

Forgiveness is a choice.

Forgiveness is our choice. It is not dependent on circumstances or another human being. Our offender's behavior has no power over us. Even when those who hurt us are not sorry for the pain they caused, we can still forgive them. We are the freed ones. Debbie Sawyer, a victim of childhood abuse, says, "Forgiveness only takes one." We forgive because we have been forgiven and follow God.

Forgiveness is impossible apart from God.

True forgiveness is a miracle. It is impossible to experience authentic healing apart from God. Forgiveness is unnatural. Seeking revenge is our natural human response. Seeking the best for someone who harmed us is a miraculous act. We are most Christlike when we forgive.

The path of forgiveness is not intended to be walked alone.

Forgiveness is a difficult process, requiring hard work and sacrifice. We need the support of friends, loving family, and often professional counselors to help us honestly look at our pain before letting it go. Forgiveness is a courageous act, made easier by the comfort of those who care about us.

Forgiveness is tangible.

Forgiveness is tangible action beyond mere words. When Paul made his appeal for Onesimus, the runaway slave, he offered to personally pay back anything Onesimus owed (Philemon 18).

When we forgive, we give up the right to get even. We pray for our offender. We want God's healing touch for the person who hurt us. Rape victims, families of murdered relatives, and others who have been victimized by criminals agree that it is hard to harbor hatred while praying for the criminal. Lee Ezell, author of *The Missing Piece*, writes:

> I knew if I didn't forgive the man who raped me as a teenager that I would be victimized by that experience my entire life. Jesus tells us to forgive those who trespass against us and this rapist literally trespassed against me. Forgiveness is God being Himself in us. God cannot change our past but He changes the effects in our lives. Forgiveness is the key to unlocking the past's hold on us. God has not left us comfortless.

Dietrich Bonhoeffer said, "Through prayer we go to our enemy, stand by his side, and plead for him to God. Jesus does not promise that when we bless our enemies and do good to them, they will not use and persecute us. They certainly will." Bonhoeffer was executed by the Nazis.

Henri Nouwen describes forgiveness as the ultimate act of generosity without limits. He says, "I might be willing to forgive but God wants me to give on top of that!"

Forgiveness heals the forgiver.

Forgiveness is the key to healing and being freed from our prison of pain. Forgiveness stops our abuser from having any power over our lives. We choose to stop being sabotaged by past events. Forgiveness comes full circle when we are healed to help others. Instead of being paralyzed and consumed with rage, we can reach out to others who experience similar suffering and offer them hope. Lewis Smedes states, "When we genuinely forgive, we set a prisoner free and then discover that the prisoner we set free was us."

> Love your enemies, do good to those who hate you, bless those who curse you, pray for those who mistreat you. If someone strikes you on one cheek, turn to him the other also. If someone takes your cloak, do not stop him from taking your tunic. Give to everyone who asks you, and if anyone takes what belongs to you, do not demand it back. Do to others as you would have them do to you.
>
> If you love those who love you, what credit is that to you? (Luke 6:27–31 NIV).

While many people struggle with thorns rooted in their past, especially forgiving their parents, some struggle with forgiving their children. These parents have given their children a secure, loving Christian home, and yet these young people make terrifying choices. One mother explains:

> Our son, Brett, began dabbling in drugs in eighth grade. He had learning disabilities and reminded me of my brother, who suffered with chemical imbalances and addiction. The nightmare continued through Brett's high school years with police arrests and a progressive addiction to drugs and alcohol. He was even caught dealing drugs. My husband and I would lie awake many weekend nights because he never

came home. As committed Christian parents, we engaged every possible resource to help our son with his problems.

After high school, Brett became involved with Karen, an unstable young woman. She had a history of violence and was once hospitalized in a psychiatric facility. Karen was soon pregnant with Brett's child. She was unpredictable and dangerous. Sometimes Karen would rage against Brett, damaging cars and breaking windshields, and physically hurt him. We could not convince Brett to end his relationship with her.

After our grandson, Michael, was born, we remained involved with Karen, because she was Michael's mother. She was unable to care for him. Through many court battles and legal proceedings, we were able to become Michael's guardians. We are raising him. Brett has little contact with Karen now. Karen sporadically contacts Michael, which confuses him.

I forgave Karen for the chaos she caused our family, and I continue to daily forgive my son and love him completely without condition. His addiction problems continued. He was driving under the influence one night and flipped the car, severely injuring his friend in the passenger seat. If his friend had died, Brett would have been convicted of manslaughter. Brett's friend lived, but Brett was sent to jail. In a letter from jail, he wrote, "I'm sorry for all the hell I've put you through. Thank you for always loving me and standing by me."

> Forgiveness has been the key to my preservation.
> Forgiveness opens the door and compassion walks through it.
>
> —Chuck Lynch

Pain Clinic

- Read Luke 6:27–37. Loving and forgiving our enemies is not optional.

- If we understand that God's goal is for us to become Christ-like, then forgiveness is our prime opportunity to reflect Jesus Christ. Think about your experiences with forgiveness, when you have forgiven someone as well as having been forgiven by someone else.

- How did the principles about what is and is not forgiveness in this chapter apply to your experiences?

> No sacrifice which a lover would make for his beloved is too great for us to make for our enemy.
>
> —Dietrich Bonhoeffer

We must finally be reconciled with our foe, lest we both perish in the vicious circle of hatred.

—Reinhold Niebuhr

Love's power to forgive is stronger than hate's power to get even.

—Lewis Smedes

Forgiveness is the way to step over the wall and welcome others into my heart without expecting anything in return. Maybe the authentic discipline of forgiveness is more "climbing over" than "stepping over."

—Henri Nouwen

Forgiving the unforgivable

Then Peter came to Jesus and asked, "Lord, how many times shall I forgive my brother when he sins against me? Up to seven times?"
Jesus answered, "I tell you, not seven times, but seventy-seven times."

Matthew 18:21–22 NIV

Principles of forgiveness are empty without real-life examples and practice. This chapter is a challenging exercise in practicing forgiveness. As you read through the following experiences, ask yourself if you could practice forgiveness in each case. While interviewing forgivers and reading other accounts of forgiveness, I came to the conclusion that I honestly don't know if I could forgive the offenses that some of them forgave. Several of these stories are presented as composites, combining multiple examples. Between sections are placed Scripture references about forgiveness to help us face the reality of God's command.

> Forgiveness is only real for him who has discovered the weakness of his friends and the sins of his enemy in his own heart and is willing to call every human being his brother.
>
> —Henri Nouwen

Forgiving Betrayal

Wes learned that his wife was having an affair with his best friend. Through God's healing, with the help of marriage counseling, Wes and his wife restored their marriage, but it was far more difficult for Wes to forgive his former best friend. He had known this friend since childhood and was now no longer speaking to him. Several years later, Wes realized that his rage over the betrayal continued to poison his relationships. Wes met with his former best friend to forgive him in person and restore their friendship.

> Get rid of all bitterness, rage and anger, brawling and slander, along with every form of malice. Be kind and compassionate to one another, forgiving each other, just as in Christ God forgave you.
>
> Ephesians 4:31–32 NIV

One betrayed wife said, "Forgiveness is giving up one's perceived right to hold a sin over another person's head." She learned that her husband was having an affair with her best friend, the wife of a close relative. They separated, and she contemplated divorce. This wife wanted to punish her husband for being unfaithful and destroying their entire family. Both couples began the long process of counseling, forgiveness, and reconciliation. Today they spend family holidays together. They learned that forgiveness is God's command, not a suggestion. It is an act of the will not based on feelings.

> Bear with each other and forgive whatever grievances you may have against one another. Forgive as the Lord forgave you. And over all these virtues put on love, which binds them all together in perfect unity.
>
> Colossians 3:13–14 NIV

When Stephanie married Mark, she longed for the ideal family life she never had as a child. Mark seemed to come from the perfect intact Christian family. She learned years later that he was a sex addict, frequenting pornography shops and prostitutes. Stephanie took her marriage vows seriously; she was committed through "sickness and health." Mark entered therapy for his addiction, and the couple also saw a marriage counselor. Stephanie and Mark separated to protect their children and continued to work on their marriage. After several attempts at reconciliation, Stephanie realized that Mark's behavior would never change. She prayed for Mark's healing and forgave him for the years of heartache and misery he caused, but she could no longer subject herself to his addiction.

> Jesus said, "Father, forgive them, for they do not know what they are doing." And they divided up his clothes by casting lots.
>
> Luke 23:34 NIV

Forgiving Abuse

Debbie Sawyer still suffers from injuries caused by the beatings she received from her mother. Debbie and her three sisters were physically abused and constantly told that they were stupid and worthless. Their one brother lived unscathed in their home. Worse than their mother's beatings and verbal abuse was the sexual molestation the sisters endured from their father. Only later in life did Debbie and her sisters learn that their father had abused each of them. Debbie's father also molested her best friend. When Debbie witnessed him molesting a cousin, she finally threatened to expose him, and her father threatened to kill her. Then he ignored her.

Through attending a local church and being discipled by the pastor and his family, Debbie came to know God, a loving father so different from her earthly one. She attended a Baptist college in another state, her tuition funded by the church. Debbie's parents did not attend her graduation, her wedding to her college sweetheart, or the birth of her daughter. She rarely heard from them.

Years later, after studying the story of Joseph (Genesis 37–50), Debbie realized that she needed to forgive her parents, especially her father. She related to the brutal abuse Joseph suffered at the hands of his brothers. Debbie was struck that when Joseph had the perfect opportunity for revenge, he kissed his brothers, embraced them, and spoke kindly to each one. Joseph provided for his brothers and their families during the famine. Debbie decided to make the most difficult phone call of her life. Forgiveness is a decision and a choice. This phone call changed her life:

Debbie:	"Dad, I know what you did to me as a child."
Debbie's father:	"I don't know what you are talking about."
Debbie:	"I think that you do."
Debbie's father:	"Well, I have forgotten all about it, so why don't you do the same?"
Debbie:	"Dad, I have not forgotten, and I know you haven't forgotten either. I know about my

	sisters, my cousin, and my best friend. But I am calling about you and me."
Debbie's father:	(silence)
Debbie:	"Dad, I think you know why I haven't been home. I can't be in the same room with you. I don't understand why you would hurt me. Sometimes I have been so angry with you. But I am calling today to tell you that I forgive you. Did you hear me, Dad? I forgive you for what you did to me."
Debbie's father:	"Yes."

Debbie's phone call with her dad ended. She felt as if fifty pounds had been lifted from her. She felt completely free. Years later, when her father was hospitalized and lay dying, she visited him, feeling compassion for his brokenness. He died, and a few years later her mother died, never having taken responsibility for abusing her children. Debbie's mother had often said that she wouldn't change one thing about their childhoods. Debbie also forgave her mother.

Debbie longed for her parents to ask for her forgiveness and seek reconciliation, but that never occurred. Debbie learned that forgiveness only takes one. Joseph's brothers never asked for forgiveness, yet Joseph forgave them and blessed them. As Debbie began to heal and experience God's miraculous gift of forgiveness, she started teaching Bible studies and had opportunities to speak at Christian conferences on the topic of forgiveness. She continues to tell other women who have experienced unforgivable abuse that forgiveness heals the forgiver, and they can be free.

> "I am your brother Joseph whom you sold into Egypt.
> But now, do not grieve, do not reproach yourselves for

> having sold me here, since God sent me before you to preserve your lives . . ."
>
> Then throwing his arms around the neck of his brother Benjamin he [Joseph] wept; and Benjamin wept on his shoulder. He kissed all his brothers, weeping over them.
>
> Genesis 45:4–6, 14–15 TJB

Ultimate Forgiveness

> If God can forgive a serial killer, maybe there's hope for us all.
>
> —Martin R. De Haan II

Rick forgave the man who shot and murdered his son. He visits this criminal on death row and has led him to Jesus Christ. Lynn and Justin forgave the teenage drunk driver who was responsible for the death of their daughter. He never served jail time and remains unrepentant about the accident. When Susie was kidnapped, her mother said in an interview:

> I came to the point where I was paralyzed and consumed with rage. I wanted brutal revenge. But I knew this hatred would destroy me, my faith, and my family. I didn't know if my seven-year-old daughter was dead or alive. Then I began to daily pray for her kidnapper. I began the long journey of forgiving him for the unspeakable horror he had inflicted on our family.

Forgiveness is not forgetting. It is not a feeling. It doesn't make sense. True miraculous forgiveness is impossible apart from God. Forgiveness is a choice, a tangible process. Through closely examining the root of our pain and forgiving the person who wounded us, we unlock the chains that imprison us. Forgiveness heals and frees the forgiver. We can forgive someone who is not sorry. While reconciliation depends on two people, forgiveness depends only on one.

> Forgive us our debts,
> as we also have forgiven our debtors.
> And lead us not into temptation,
> but deliver us from the evil one.
>
> For if you forgive men when they sin against you, your heavenly Father will also forgive you. But if you do not forgive men their sins, your Father will not forgive your sins.
>
> Matthew 6:12–15 NIV

Forgiving Yourself

> Even though I was once a blasphemer and a persecutor and a violent man, I was shown mercy because I acted in ignorance and unbelief. The grace of our Lord was poured out on me abundantly, along with the faith and love that are in Christ Jesus.
>
> Here is a trustworthy saying that deserves full acceptance: Christ Jesus came into the world to save sinners—of whom I am the worst. But for that very reason I was shown mercy so that in me, the worst of sinners, Christ Jesus might display his unlimited patience as an example for those who would believe on him and receive eternal life.
>
> 1 Timothy 1:13–16 NIV

Paul understood what it felt like to be the worst of all sinners. He persecuted and killed Christians. He approved the stoning of

Stephen (Acts 8:1). Paul blasphemed against God. He knew that his life resonated, "If God can forgive me, He can forgive anyone."

Often more difficult than forgiving others is forgiving ourselves. We are the harshest of judges, constantly reminding ourselves of our failures. We feel that we do not deserve forgiveness. ***Survival step #8*** is to forgive yourself. One recovering alcoholic explains:

> Abused in my childhood by alcoholic parents, I became an alcoholic later in life. I learned from my parents that drugs and alcohol numbed the pain. Through a long process of recovery, I am clean and sober today. Letting go of the past required forgiveness. I had to bring every horrible memory out into the open, look at it, accept it, and let it go. That was the key to my healing. I began to grieve for my family and feel compassion for them, understanding the pain that trapped them. Harder than forgiving the people in my past has been forgiving myself. I am the only one responsible for my adult behavior and continuing the cycle. As an alcoholic, I inflicted the same pain on my wife and children that my parents inflicted on me. But I can forgive myself because Jesus forgives me. I have learned that we are only as gracious and merciful to others as we are to ourselves.

Forgiving ourselves and forgiving others is a linked process, impossible before we fully embrace God's forgiveness. Lydia grew up with a distant father and an alcoholic mother who beat her. Desperate for love as a young adult, she became involved with different men, sometimes married men. When she became pregnant, she avoided the problem with an abortion. She lived her life, blocking out the past and future, until her pain became unbearable, and she considered suicide. Only when she began to fully understand God's forgiveness was she able to forgive her parents and finally forgive herself.

> Miracle of miracles, you can forgive yourself because you are forgiven, accept yourself because you are accepted, and begin to start building up the very places you once tore down. There is grace to help in every time of trouble. That grace is the secret to being able to forgive ourselves.
>
> —John Claypool

Robert was starting his car with his sons in the back seat. He didn't realize that the back passenger door was not secure and his young son had fallen out of the car. The car rolled forward and crushed the boy's head. Robert's son was dead before they reached the hospital. Robert's wife became overwhelmed with grief and despair and couldn't leave her bed. Robert felt equally overwhelmed with grief and guilt and contemplated suicide, anything to stop the intense pain. Yet Robert knew that he could not cause his family more grief and pain. He blamed himself for his son's death. He survived only because he clung to God's promises of forgiveness and eternal life.

> To forgive yourself takes high courage . . . and you dare forgive yourself only with the courage of love. It takes a miracle of love to get rid of the unforgiving inquisitor lurking in the shadows of your heart. To forgive your own self is the ultimate miracle of healing.
>
> —Lewis Smedes

Scriptural Unforgivable Acts

If you want to wrestle with unforgivable acts in Scripture, read 2 Samuel 11–13. David committed adultery and murder, manipulating circumstances to protect himself. He lusted after another man's wife (Bathsheba), slept with her, and used his power to have her husband murdered. David's actions resulted in the death of the son he conceived with Bathsheba.

Amnon, David's son, raped Tamar, his sister. Amnon was obsessed with Tamar; his desire made him feel ill. Amnon tricked Tamar into bringing food to him in his bed, feigning sickness. When Tamar tried to stop him from raping her, Amnon overpowered her and then only felt hatred for her. When King David heard that Tamar had been violated, he was quite angry, but he did not punish Amnon: "When King David heard the whole story, he was very angry; but he had no wish to harm his son Amnon, since he loved him; he was his first-born. Absalom however would not so much as speak to Amnon, for he hated Amnon for having raped his sister Tamar" (2 Samuel 13:21–22 TJB).

First-born Amnon received preferential treatment from David. He was only walking in his father's footsteps. David was not a common criminal, though he acted like one, but a king who trusted God. David was a man who clung to God's forgiveness. Consumed with lust, manipulative, and willing to rape and murder, these men deserved execution. Could you have forgiven any of these acts committed against your family, especially committed by those claiming to follow God?

Absalom could not forgive Amnon and arranged to have him murdered. He then fled. Absalom was later killed by Joab, one of David's advisors, despite David's request that Absalom's life be spared. David was overcome with grief when he learned of Absalom's death: "The king shuddered. He went up to the room over the gate and burst into tears, and weeping said, 'My son Absalom! My son! My son Absalom! Would I had died in your place! Absalom, my son, my son!' " (2 Samuel 19:1–2 TJB).

Being unforgiving, grief, hatred, lust, and violent crime are some of the human patterns that Jesus, God's only Son, came to free us from. Embracing God's forgiveness for ourselves and others is the key to healing.

> All of us can identify things we wish we had done differently, our mistakes and unwise decisions. But we cannot confidently face the future if we are locked in regret.
>
> —Gordon T. Smith

Pain Clinic

- Read Hosea 3 about forgiving the adulterous spouse. Read Luke 15:11–31 about forgiving the prodigal son. This is how God views us. We are the unfaithful spouse and rebellious child. Yet God compassionately welcomes us home.

- Think about your experiences with:
  forgiving yourself
  forgiving someone who is not sorry
  forgiving an unforgivable act

  Were you able to repay evil with a blessing? Have you struggled with forgiving someone? Has this been an obstacle to surviving your thorns?

> Do not repay evil with evil or insult with insult, but with blessing, because to this you were called so that you may inherit a blessing.
>
> 1 Peter 3:9 NIV

You have been wounded in many ways. The more you open yourself to being healed, the more you will discover how deep your wounds are. You will be tempted to become discouraged, because under every wound you uncover you will find others. Your search for true healing will be a suffering search. Many tears still need to be shed.

But do not be afraid. The simple fact that you are more aware of your wounds shows that you have sufficient strength to face them.

—Henri Nouwen

When we refuse to compare ourselves to one another, when we reject envy and jealousy of others, of their gifts and abilities and opportunities, we are freed to be who we are.

—Gordon T. Smith

Taming the MONSTERS OF Envy and Resentment

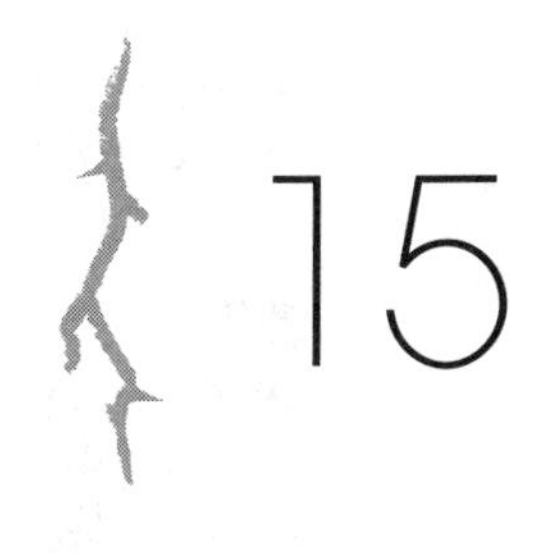

The life of the body is a tranquil heart,
but envy is a cancer in the bones.
Proverbs 14:30 TJB

We know that we should not withhold forgiveness or "pay back wrong for wrong." We must refrain from paying back evil for evil or insult with insult (1 Peter 3:8b–9). Instead God wants us to repay evil with a blessing, the most powerful witness possible of His unconditional love. Making the effort to bless someone who wounded us in tangible ways is ultimate forgiveness.

Along with being unforgiving and seeking revenge lie other insidious monsters: envy, bitterness, jealousy, and resentment. When we live with thorns, we are especially vulnerable to these monsters. While wrestling with forgiveness usually involves someone who hurt us, wrestling with envy and resentment often involves people who may not have hurt us. They simply represent a life we do not live; they have something that we long to possess. God asks us to also bless people who we resent because we feel envious.

Envy and jealousy are quite different. Envy is defined as "the painful or resentful awareness of an advantage enjoyed by another joined with a desire to possess the same advantage." Jealousy is defined as "being intolerant of rivalry or unfaithfulness." Jealousy can be an appropriate, healthy emotion. Most spouses would feel jealous upon learning their husband or wife was considering an extramarital affair. We have a jealous God who does not tolerate our serving other idols (Exodus 20:4–5): "You shall have no gods except me" (Exodus 20:3 TJB).

Envy and resentment are unhealthy emotions. Unchecked, they can take root and cause deep bitterness. Bitterness can lead to a hardening of our hearts against God and others. Envy is wanting what someone else has and being discontent with what God has given us, whether it be our resources, physical bodies, spouses, families, gifts and talents, careers, ministries, or any aspect of our lives. James 3:16 (NIV) says, "Where you have envy and selfish ambition, there you find disorder and every evil practice." Proverbs 14:30 says that envy is like a cancer in our bones. Cancerous cells multiply out of control. We may require spiritual radiation and chemotherapy treatment. ***Survival step #9*** is to tame our monsters of envy, resentment, and bitterness.

> My feet had almost slipped,
> my foothold had all but given way,
> because the boasts of sinners roused my envy
> when I saw how they prosper.
> No pain, no suffering is theirs;
> they are sleek and sound in limb;
> they are not plunged in trouble as other men are,
> nor do they suffer the torments of mortal men. (Psalm 73:2–5 NEB)

The psalmist sees that the wicked are arrogant and becoming rich. They are healthy and do not seem to suffer. The psalmist's envy is causing him to stumble. Later he realizes that God is all he wants or needs:

> When my heart was embittered
> I felt the pangs of envy,
> I would not understand, so brutish was I,
> I was a mere beast in thy sight, O God.
> Yet I am always with thee,
> thou holdest my right hand;
> thou dost guide me by thy counsel
> and afterwards wilt receive me with glory.
> Whom have I in heaven but thee?
> And having thee, I desire nothing else on earth.
> Though heart and body fail,
> yet God is my possession for ever. (Psalm 73:21–26 NEB)

Psalm 73 deals with envy head on. While people who do not follow God may be successful and healthy, we have God holding us by the hand, guiding us. We have a heavenly hope. Though our hearts and bodies may fail, we have God forever. How could we desire anything else?

But we do desire something else. In *The Memory Keeper's Daughter* by Kim Edwards, the main character kneels at his sister's grave, overcome with grief. He begins to recite Psalm 23: The Lord is my shepherd; I shall not want. "But I do want, Lord," he cries out. We understand. There is so much that we want on this side of eternity. We may not want the "riches of the wicked," but we may want the hug of a loved one who is deceased, a peaceful marriage, or a happy child. Yes, we want.

Why Me?

A friend, one who has endured more than his fair share of suffering, recently asked me about the topic of this book. I explained that it was about living with unchanged circumstances. He laughed and asked, "Unchanged circumstances for people with tough lives, or unchanged circumstances for people who lead ideal lives?" That's a good question. If we are completely honest, most Christians do not seriously struggle with envying people who do not follow God. We would not want to be on that path. We do struggle with envying other believers who seem to be richly blessed by God, who never face significant suffering. We feel like children on Christmas morning observing some of our siblings opening a bounty of desired gifts while we receive only one small present, not something that we longed for or would have chosen. We wonder, "Why not us, Lord? Why do we have to suffer and not them?" Wouldn't the fair, just approach be that we all suffer a similar amount?

Tanya and her husband, Alex, have longed to have a baby for years. When medical intervention did not help Tanya conceive, she and Alex began exploring adoption. It has been a costly process with no results so far. They remain hopeful that God will someday give them a child. Yet Tanya struggles when she reads about an unwed teenage mother who aborted her baby or leaves an infant to die in a trash can. She struggles when her friends become pregnant easily. Tanya envies her sister, who has four children. She doesn't understand God's ways. She wonders on bad days, "If children are a blessing from God, has God chosen not to bless me?"

Lisa envies her best friend's marriage, the ideal relationship that Lisa does not share with her difficult husband. Renee's daughter has bipolar disorder and abuses drugs and alcohol. Renee grieves when she hears about a friend's high-achieving child who has just been accepted to a prestigious university. Maureen's chronic illness makes it difficult to get out of bed every morning. She tires in a few hours and is in pain most of the day. Her close friend runs in marathons and seems to have boundless energy. Her visits only leave Maureen feeling more inadequate and despairing.

Of course, we envy people who have the life we want. We are human like the disciples. They were envious of one another, arguing about which one of them was the greatest (Luke 22:24–26). The disciples perceived that one of them would be preferred over the others. Jesus told them, "But you are not to be like that" (v. 26 NIV).

The disciples were keeping score. Sometimes we measure our life against someone else's life and we keep score too.

> But if you harbor bitter envy and selfish ambition in your hearts, do not boast about it or deny the truth. Such "wisdom" does not come down from heaven but is earthly, unspiritual, of the devil. For where you have envy and selfish ambition, there you find disorder and every evil practice.
>
> James 3:14–16 NIV

Pain Clinic

- In *The Five People You Meet in Heaven*, Mitch Albom describes anger as a poison that eats us from inside and hatred as a curved blade that harms us. Being unforgiving and having anger, hatred, and envy are self-inflicted wounds. How have you harmed yourself with these unhealthy emotions?

- Read Mark 4:18–19 (NIV) as a thorns survivor: "Still others, like seed sown among thorns, hear the word . . . the desires for other things come in and choke the word, making it unfruitful."

> Do not worry about the wicked,
> Do not envy those who do wrong.
>
> Be quiet before Yahweh, and wait patiently for him,
> Not worrying about men who make their fortunes.
>
> Psalm 37:1, 7 TJB

What is the antidote for envy? It is being quiet before God and waiting on Him. We are not to worry about the success of others or envy them. Practice this focus on God the next time your monsters of envy and resentment rear their heads.

> You want something which you cannot have, and so you are bent on murder; you are envious, and cannot attain your ambition, and so you quarrel and fight . . . Whoever chooses to be the world's friend makes himself God's enemy.

Or do you suppose that Scripture has no meaning when it says that the spirit which God implanted in man turns towards envious desires? And yet the grace he gives is stronger.

James 4:2a, 5 NEB

Our work is never the primary expression of our identity, and through regular Sabbath rest we re-establish our identity in God and in his love.

—Gordon T. Smith

God does not want you to destroy yourself. Exhaustion, burnout, and depression are not signs that you are doing God's will.

—Henri Nouwen

Then (Jesus) said to them, "The Sabbath was made for man, not man for the Sabbath. So the Son of Man is Lord even of the Sabbath."

Mark 2:27–28 (NIV)

Taking Care of Ourselves: Finding True Rest

God rarely, if ever, calls us to be or to do so much that we must sacrifice the fundamental relationships of our lives or neglect our need for sleep, rest, friendship, worship, and recreation.

—Gordon T. Smith

During our time in the pain clinic so far, we have practiced forgiving others and ourselves, and we have worked on taming our monsters of envy and resentment. The next steps may surprise you. ***Survival step #10*** can be summarized like this: Take good care of yourself. This approach may even seem unbiblical. Aren't we supposed to focus on caring for others before ourselves? Yes.

But if we do not care for ourselves as God instructed, we will not have the resources we need to reach out to others, especially difficult people that God places in our lives. First things first. Take good care of yourself and find complete rest.

The history of the word *good* shows that it is closely related to God. For example, *good-bye* originally meant "God be with you." Instead of making it a priority to "take good care of yourself," focus on "taking godly care of yourself." This step is especially critical for those of us who live with thorns. God gives us specific guidance in Scripture about caring for ourselves. Consider these principles the "spa" of the Bible. The most important principle is finding rest. Other ways to care for yourself will follow in the next chapter.

> These are the words of the Lord: Stop at the crossroads; look for the ancient paths; ask, 'Where is the way that leads to what is good?' Then take that way, and you will find rest for yourselves. But they said, 'We will not.'
>
> Jeremiah 6:16 NEB

Finding Rest

> Remember the sabbath day and keep it holy. For six days you shall labor and do all your work, but the seventh day is a sabbath for Yahweh your God. You shall do no work that day.
>
> Exodus 20:8–9 TJB

God intends for us to seek and find rest, completely focusing on Him without distraction. This act replenishes our resources.

> If you refrain from trampling the sabbath,
> and doing business on the holy day,
> if you call the sabbath "Delightful,"
> and the day sacred to Yahweh "Honorable,"

> if you honor it by abstaining from travel,
> from doing business and from gossip,
> then shall you find your happiness in Yahweh
> and I will lead you triumphant over the heights of the
> land. (Isaiah 58:13 TJB)

Numerous Scripture verses command us to observe the Sabbath, and yet it remains one of the most misunderstood practices. Most people think that observing the Sabbath is attending church on Sunday (or Saturday night). Observing the Sabbath can include going to church, but sometimes we miss the point. Living in our overextended, exhausted culture affects our ability to understand true rest.

The Jews in Jesus' day also missed the point: "It was works of this kind done on the Sabbath that stirred the Jews to persecute Jesus" (John 5:16 NEB).

The Jews were offended and angry that Jesus healed people on the Sabbath. When Jesus healed a man who had been crippled for thirty-eight years, Jesus told the man, "Take up your bed and walk." It was a momentous, exciting occasion for this man to be able to carry his own bed and walk. The Jews told this cured man that he was not allowed to carry his bed on the Sabbath (John 5:10). They were imprisoned by legalism, following the letter of the law without understanding the spirit of the law. They followed the rules of Sabbath without understanding its true purpose. It is no wonder that Jesus became livid and violent when he found men transacting business in the temple, the home of the Sabbath (Matthew 21:12–13).

Weary Servants

> Come to me, all you who are weary and burdened, and
> I will give you rest.
>
> Matthew 11:28 NIV

For over thirty years, my husband and I were involved in church music ministry. We worked at three different churches through the decades. My husband was the music minister, and I was the church pianist and choral accompanist. Sometimes I worked with children's groups. A typical Sunday included two to three services (sometimes evening services); separate rehearsals for adult, youth, and children's choirs; and additional planning meetings. Sometimes my husband taught Sunday school classes. I helped with other church programs. Depending on seasonal events, such as major Christmas or Easter musicals, we also had multiple rehearsals during the week and on Saturdays.

We never experienced a Sabbath day, and Sunday was the busiest day of the week. As our family grew and my husband's job required him to travel more frequently, it became clear that my husband's leadership of a music ministry was unrealistic. After our dismissal, we went to church and sat in a pew for the first time in our married life. We enjoyed the luxury of visiting other churches. We began to experience the Sabbath and focused on God. We worshiped Him without distraction or overwhelming responsibilities. My husband is a natural leader, so this change was initially a difficult transition for him. He was no longer in charge. God was in charge.

Scripture supports the view that those who lead worship should be experiencing a heightened Sabbath experience. Yet often that is not the case. We unintentionally trample the Sabbath. We conduct church business. If you have numerous responsibilities at your church and Sunday is one of the busiest days of the week, you should continue to follow a legitimate calling from God, but you need to find another way to experience the Sabbath, a time of rest to reconnect with God. Pastors certainly experience Sabbath on another day of the week.

You may also plan your retreat time on another day of the week. You might go for early morning walks, having deep conversations with God. You may block out a specific time of the day to observe a daily Sabbath. The key elements are worshiping God, reading His Word (love letters to you), communicating with Him without distraction, and resting from work and your daily grind. Sabbath is our time to be immersed in our intimate love relationship with God. Lovers who spend time together are not distracted or too busy to focus on their partner; likewise, we want to focus on God, the Lover of our souls.

> I gave them my laws and taught them my observances, which must be practiced by all who want to live. I even gave them my sabbaths to be a sign between me and them, so that they might learn that I, Yahweh, am the one who sanctifies them. The House of Israel, however, rebelled against me in the wilderness; they refused to keep my laws, they scorned my observances, which must be practiced by all who wish to live, and they profaned my sabbaths.
>
> Ezekiel 20:11–13 TJB

Gordon Smith describes the Sabbath as an intentional break designed to bring balance to a person's life. The Sabbath was intended to be God's gift to us. He sanctifies us, cleansing us and setting us apart for a sacred purpose. This is our true sanctuary, a place of protection and refuge. If your current Sabbath experience leaves you drained and exhausted, you are not observing the Sabbath that God intended, one that reenergizes you.

> You must keep my sabbaths carefully, because the sabbath is a sign between myself and you from generation to generation to show that it is I, Yahweh, who sanctify you.
>
> Exodus 31:12–13 TJB

Leaving Your Burdens Behind

Observing a Sabbath retreat has three more requirements. The first requirement is that we leave our burdens behind:

> "Yahweh says this: As you value your lives, on no account carry a burden on the Sabbath day or bring it in through the gates of Jerusalem. Bring no burden out of your houses on the sabbath day, and do no work. Keep the sabbath day holy, as I commanded your ancestors" (Jeremiah 17:21–22 TJB).

We carry our burdens and thorns every day of our lives. Jeremiah may have been referring to actual physical burdens or mental ones. If we "value our lives," we must lay these burdens down to find rest. We will not survive if we do not learn to regularly take a break from our life challenges.

When we stop focusing on our burdens, we can remember how God cares for us. We can remember the miracles He has done in our lives and will continue to do.

> Observe the sabbath day and keep it holy, as Yahweh your God has commanded you. For six days you shall labor and do all your work, but the seventh day is a sabbath for Yahweh your God. You shall do no work that day, neither you nor your son nor your daughter nor your servants, men or women, nor your ox nor your donkey nor any of your animals, nor the stranger who lives with you. Thus your servant, man or woman, shall rest as you do. *Remember* that you were a servant in the land of Egypt, and that Yahweh your God brought you out from there with mighty hand and outstretched arm; because of this, Yahweh your God has commanded you to keep the sabbath day.
>
> Deuteronomy 5:12–15 TJB,
> emphasis added.

Our burdens become overwhelming when we forget who God is and what He can accomplish in our lives. The antidote is remembering. The second requirement of observing a Sabbath retreat is to spend time remembering that God's mighty hand and outstretched arm rest on our shoulder.

The third requirement is observing a day of complete rest, not partial rest: "This is Yahweh's command: Tomorrow is a day of complete rest, a sabbath sacred to Yahweh. Bake what you want to bake, boil what you want to boil; put aside all that is left for tomorrow" (Exodus 16:23 TJB).

God's people were instructed not even to cook on the Sabbath. They could eat leftovers. The complete day of rest was commanded for everyone—not just a select group. Not even servants or animals were allowed to work. The day of retreat was a command, not an optional activity.

Jesus understood the critical role of rest in ministry: "The apostles gathered around Jesus and reported to him all they had done and taught. Then, because so many people were coming and going that they did not even have a chance to eat, he said to them, 'Come with me by yourselves to a quiet place and get some rest'" (Mark 6:30–31 NIV).

Jesus and His disciples needed time to rest by themselves, eat, and be replenished. After they rested, Jesus fed the five thousand. Jesus calls to us today, "Come by yourself to a quiet place and get some rest." Your place and time of rest may occur in a church service. Your Sabbath retreat may fall on Sunday. Yet for many believers, the two do not mix. Should my husband and I have been involved in music ministry for thirty years? Yes. I do believe that God called us to do that, and we have observed the impact it had on numerous lives. Scripture also teaches how important it is for believers to gather together to worship Him and encourage one another (Hebrews 10:25). But did my husband and I observe the Sabbath retreat that God intended on the seventh day? Of course not. In hindsight, I realize that we needed to diligently build a different type of Sabbath experience into our days.

A Time for Pampering

In addition to feeling rested, God also wants us to feel pampered when we need encouragement. In Nehemiah 8:1–12, Ezra is reading the Book of the Law to men, women, and children (old enough to understand) from early morning till noon. This event follows the building of the walls of Jerusalem, so the people moved from construction to instruction. After hours of listening, the people are in tears. They are probably physically and emotionally overwhelmed and exhausted. Imagine how tired the children are. Nehemiah and Ezra know that it's time for a break. They tell the people: "This day is sacred to Yahweh your God. Do not be mournful, do not weep . . . Go, eat the fat, drink the sweet wine, and send a portion to the man who has nothing prepared ready. For this day is sacred to our Lord. Do not be sad: the joy of Yahweh is your stronghold" (Nehemiah 8:9–10 TJB). Good leaders know when their followers need to enjoy a break and be pampered and rewarded. This is God's intent for our Sabbath retreat. We are to work hard, but we are also to revel in God's love and pampering. Lest we think that this is a self-consumed pampering, note that we are told to provide pampering for others who do not have our resources: "Send a portion to the man who has nothing prepared already." We are to be generous with what God has provided.

Solitude and Silence

> Too often the church is an enemy of our solitude. Too often the church is one more agent in the vast social conspiracy of togetherness and noise aimed at distracting us from encountering ourselves.
>
> —Parker Palmer

Solitude and silence play critical roles in our Sabbath experience. These practices have never been more important than they are today in our age of technological bombardment and unrelenting input. John White says that Satan wants our world to be as noisy as possible to block out God's voice.

Addiction to stress and constant activity is an actual disorder, not only life-threatening to our bodies but also to relationships. Anhedonia is a state of numbness or depression resulting from an addiction to over-stimulating and thrilling experiences. Archibald Hart, seminary professor, psychologist, and author of *Thrilled to Death*, is concerned that pastors and others in ministry are especially vulnerable to this addiction. He's not surprised that an increasing number of pastors have succumbed to sexual temptation. Those who suffer with anhedonia no longer find joy in the mundane, simple pleasures of life but need intensely exciting experiences to feel alive. Our culture fuels this addiction.

Solitude and silence are intolerable for people who struggle with stress addiction. Facing seasons of isolation is foreign to us. Too many despairing people seem to be experiencing God's silence (as discussed in chapter 7), but often God is gently whispering, and we can't hear Him. Frederick Buechner says that prayer can be conversations with God scattered throughout the day, but more important is prayer that is deeply silent, watching and listening for God to speak. Listening is a critical part of prayer, but we are out of practice.

Before technology took such a place of prominence in our culture, times of solitude, reflection, and prayer were naturally built into our days, during experiences such as taking walks to driving in a car. Today cell phones can invade every minute of our day. In addition to immediate access to conversation, we can also watch television shows and play games. We never have to go without non-stop input. Young people don't know the difference. Even churches, in their passion to be culturally relevant and accessible to all, have abandoned solitude and silence. When I attend my daughter's church service for young adults, I do enjoy the high energy level, contemporary music, lights show, and even snacks provided during the service. I am definitely entertained, having fun, and happy to see these young people coming to worship God. This service speaks their language. Yet there is not one moment of silence, not one chance to listen to God. When they face tough times in adulthood, will these young people understand God's use of silence and solitude in their lives? Or will they feel abandoned by Him?

> There are fewer and fewer oases of silence in our noisy world. Communication has higher value for us than contemplation. Information is in greater demand than reflection.
>
> —Barbara Brown Taylor

Pain Clinic

- Does your Sabbath recharge your batteries–or drain them? How does the church service that you attend add to or detract from your Sabbath experience?

- Try this experiment. Plan a Sabbath experience that meets the following biblical criteria:

    - You will truly rest.
    - You will focus on God without distraction.
    - You will leave your burdens behind and certainly not add to them.

- You will remember how God has cared for you in the past.
- You will not work in any way and enjoy complete rest.
- You may even pamper yourself but make sure others are being pampered too.
- Include experiences of solitude and silence.

How did this Sabbath compare with your normal Sabbath experience?

> There remains, then, a Sabbath-rest for the people of God; for anyone who enters God's rest also rests from his own work, just as God did from his. Let us, therefore, make every effort to enter that rest, so that no one will fall by following their example of disobedience.
>
> Hebrews 4:9–11 NIV

I, for my part, celebrate your strength,
I sing of your love morning by morning;
You have always been my citadel,
A shelter when I am in trouble.

Psalm 59:16 TJB

Because music penetrates deeper than words, even deeper than pain, it is curative even in the direst of situations.

—Mary Pipher

Taking GODLY CARE of ourselves 17

But by thy saving power, O God, lift me high
above my pain and my distress,
then I will praise God's name in song
and glorify him with thanksgiving.

Psalm 69:29–30 NEB

Did you know that Scripture includes over two hundred specific references directing us to make music unto the Lord? Similar to the passages about observing the Sabbath, these instructions are commands, not suggestions. *Commands* are defined as "given orders." Imagine a soldier in military service who follows orders only when he feels like it or finds it convenient. In addition to finding complete rest, God specifies two other ways to connect with Him. The first is to make music unto the Lord. If you have perceived music-making as a frill or recreational hobby or simply a segment in your church worship service—inapplicable to your life—you will be surprised to learn that this command is intended for all believers. You have denied yourself a healing gift from God.

Engaging in music experiences is one of the most powerful tools God has given us to be involved with Him. Music-making is one sign of a right relationship with God. Throughout the Old Testament, a distinct pattern emerges. When God's people returned to worshiping and obeying Him after a period of disobedience, they returned to music-making. Upon returning from exile, God's people laid the foundation of the temple and stopped to make music (Ezra 3:10–11). When Nehemiah completed the wall, God's people dedicated it with the organization of two great choirs accompanied by instruments (Nehemiah 12:27–43). Throughout the repeated rebellion and rededication of God's people in 1 and 2 Chronicles, a return to music-making consistently preceded obeying and worshiping God (2 Chronicles 29:26–30).

When David returned home from killing Goliath, the town celebrated with music-making (1 Samuel 18:6). When the ark of the covenant was brought home, David danced and sang before the Lord (2 Samuel 6:16–17). After they passed through the Red Sea and escaped the Egyptians, the Israelites danced and sang on the opposite shore (Exodus 15). When the prodigal son returned home to his father, there was a celebration with music and dancing (Luke 15:25). We and God are intended to greet each other with the same joyful response.

Healthy Music-Making

While music making is crucial to corporate spiritual health and worship, it is also part of our individual daily relationship with God. In Scripture, especially the Psalms, praising God and communicating through prayer are often linked with music-making. You cannot separate the experiences.

> He has put a new song in my mouth,
> a song of praise to our God. (Psalm 40:3a TJB)

> In the daytime may Yahweh
> command his love to come,
> and by night may his song be on my lips,
> a prayer to the God of my life! (Psalm 42:8 TJB)

> So what shall I do? I will pray with my spirit, but I will also pray with my mind; I will sing with my spirit, but I will also sing with my mind. (1 Corinthians 14:15 NIV)

While music-making undergirds our personal relationship with God, it is also one way we can support one another. Ephesians 5:19–20 (NIV) tells us to "speak to one another with psalms, hymns and spiritual songs. Sing and make music in your heart to the Lord, always giving thanks to God the Father for everything, in the name of our Lord Jesus Christ."

> Let the word of Christ dwell in you richly as you teach and admonish one another with all wisdom, and as you sing psalms, hymns and spiritual songs with gratitude in your hearts to God. And whatever you do, whether in word or deed, do it all in the name of the Lord Jesus, giving thanks to God the Father though him. (Colossians 3:16–17 NIV)

Our ministry of music to one another is also a witness to unbelievers. When Paul and Silas were singing hymns in prison, the other prisoners were listening to them (Acts 16:25). We testify to God's greatness when we sing and praise Him:

> I will sing the story of thy love, O Lord, for ever;
> I will proclaim thy faithfulness to all generations.
> (Psalm 89:1 NEB)

> Sing to him, play to him,
> tell over all his marvels! (Psalm 105:2 TJB)

God delights in responding to our music-making. His spirit participates as we praise Him with song (1 Samuel 10:5; 2 Chronicles 5:13). He even sings back to us: "The Lord your God is with you, he is mighty to save. He will take great delight in you, he will quiet you with his love, he will rejoice over you with singing" (Zephaniah 3:17).

Our Weapon

We have seen that music-making is critical to our personal and corporate spiritual health and a right relationship with God. We know that it is a tool for supporting one another and witnessing to others. Yet the power of music is most important for those of us who live with thorns. It is a weapon against our spiritual enemies and a tool that assures victory. God gives us songs in the night (Job 35:10). Psalm 71:20–23 describes the direct link between God's rescuing us from the pit of misery and hardship and our response of music-making. Martin Luther fought depression through writing music to God, and his hymns were critical to the spread of the Reformation. Many of our beloved hymns were composed by believers struggling with deep grief or afflictions. This is how they communicated with God.

Jesus understood the power that music had when He was facing trials. The last activity that He and His disciples shared before leaving for the Mount of Olives was singing a psalm together (Matthew 26:30). Paul and Silas sang hymns of praise with their feet in prison stocks (Acts 16:25). Saul found relief from his battle with depression in David's music-making (1 Samuel 16:23). Old

Testament armies often sent the choir ahead of them as they faced their enemies: "'Give praise to Yahweh,'" they sang, "'for his love is everlasting.'" As they began to sing their joy and their praise, Yahweh laid an ambush for the Ammonites and Moab and the mountain folk of Seir who had come to attack Judah, and routed them (2 Chronicles 20:2–22 TJB).

Gideon (Judges 7:16–22) and Joshua (Joshua 6:1–21) used trumpets as weapons in attacking their enemies: "On the seventh day you shall march round the city seven times and the priests shall blow their trumpets. At the blast of the rams' horns, when you hear the trumpet sound, the whole army shall raise a great shout; the wall of the city will collapse and the army shall advance, every man straight ahead" (Joshua 6:4–5 NEB). While David played the harp, an evil spirit came upon Saul, and he hurled a javelin at him, attempting to pin David to the wall. But David was able to elude Saul (1 Samuel 18:10).

Scripture teaches that music is a powerful, unbreakable, tangible link with God. Music and singing occur in God's presence (Revelation 14:2–3). When we make music to God, we can imagine our enemy putting his hands over his ears, screaming, "Make them stop singing! I can't stand that!" It should not surprise us that Scripture set to music is easy to remember or that people start singing when they are afraid.

Years ago I learned about one group of missionaries who was surrounded by cannibals. They feared for their lives and began to sing hymns about Jesus' saving power. Suddenly the cannibals ceased their crazed orgy and ran away. The native guide who was helping the missionaries found the cannibals' behavior inexplicable. Years later, those same cannibals became believers and were singing their own hymns to God.

> Because you are my help,
> I sing in the shadow of your wings.
>
> Psalm 63:7 NIV

Revelation reveals that God will remove music as a further punishment to His enemies on the final day of judgment (Revelation 18:22), but music will abound in heaven. Trumpet blasts will usher in the new age. We will be immersed in an ocean of music and praise. Our experience with music and praise here on earth is a glimpse and taste of eternity with God. Why would we deny ourselves this gift?

> You are my hiding place;
> you will protect me from trouble
> and surround me with songs of deliverance.
>
> Psalm 32:7 NIV

Survival step #11 is to make music to God. Weave that experience into your daily life. Just as some misunderstand the Sabbath to be only the day we attend church services, many Christians misunderstand praise and worship to be only a Sunday morning experience. God intends for us to engage the power of music and His presence throughout the week. Often people who do not see themselves as musically talented feel that this command does that apply to them. Some believers do sing in church choirs, play in orchestras, or participate in worship bands, but other believers can listen to music and sing praises to God while sitting in their cars in rush hour traffic. For over thirty years, I have taught music-making to children with special needs as well as adults who were wrestling with their own physical or emotional pain. Not only are praise and music our offerings to God, but this is how He blesses, pampers, and protects us. Music is a weapon. Music reinforces how we remember God's care and protection, especially when we face difficult circumstances.

> Now write down for yourselves this song and teach it to the Israelites and have them sing it, so that it may be a witness for me against them . . . And when many

> disasters and difficulties come upon them, this song will testify against them, because it will not be forgotten by their descendants. I know what they are disposed to do, even before I bring them into the land I promised them on oath." So Moses wrote down this song that day and taught it to the Israelites.
>
> Deuteronomy 31:19, 21–22 NIV

Concrete Reminders

"Now write down for yourselves this song." We have a God who uses concrete reminders to encourage us in our journey with Him, especially when "disasters and difficulties" befall us. He uses every one of our senses. He created us as people who see, touch, smell, taste, and hear. Psalm 34:8 states: "Taste and see that the Lord is good." Only in recent decades have most educators realized that children (as well as adults) need to be educated through their five senses. We each have a different learning style. The truth is that good teachers have always understood this. In 1929, Alfred North Whitehead said, "In teaching, you will come to grief as soon as you forget that your pupils have bodies." Scripture is filled with specific references to visual reminders, instructions about what we eat, musical experiences, artwork, the written word, and other concrete experiences.

> The heavens declare the glory of God,
> the vault of heaven proclaims his handiwork.
>
> Psalm 19:1 TJB

We only need to look around us at God's creation to know that God is an artist. Bezalel, artist and craftsman, was filled with the Holy Spirit (Exodus 35:30–35). Several chapters in Exodus (25–28), 1 Kings (6–7), and 2 Chronicles (3–4) offer examples of God's detailed instructions about sculpture, craftsmanship, jewel placement, embroidery, and other arts in the temple.

> You are to make a veil of purple stuffs, violet shade and red, of crimson stuffs, and of fine twined linen; you are to have it finely embroidered with cherubs. You are to hang it on four posts of acacia wood plated with gold and furnished with golden hooks and set in four silver sockets. You must hang the veil from the clasps and there behind the veil you must place the ark of the Testimony, and the veil will serve you to separate the Holy Place from the Holy of Holies. (Exodus 26:31–33 TJB)

God our Father knows that we need tangible ways to remember Him. He uses visual aids. Samuel erected a stone, calling it Ebenezer, and saying, "Thus far has Yahweh aided us" (1 Samuel 7:12 TJB). In the book of Numbers, God used tassels (15:37–38), bronze plates (16:39–40), Aaron's staff (17:10), and a bronze serpent (21:8) to provide visual reminders of His care. God gave unusually detailed instructions:

> The Lord spoke to Moses and said, Speak to the Israelites in these words: You must make tassels like flowers on the corners of your garments, you and your children's children. Into this tassel you shall work a violet thread, and whenever you see this in the tassel, you shall remember all the Lord's commands and obey them, and not go your own wanton ways, led astray by your own eyes and hearts. This token is to ensure that you remember all my commands and obey them, and keep yourselves holy, consecrated to your God. (Numbers 15:37–40 NEB)

Left to our own devices and senses, our track record as God's people is not good. We forget about God or become distracted, which often results in rebellion and disobedience. Remembering God is the key to obedience. Being in a right relationship with someone is impossible if we can't remember that person. This is why wearing a wedding ring is important. People have shared with me that when they are tempted to stray when they are away from their spouses, that wedding ring instantly reminds them of their commitment. Unmarried teens wear purity rings to remind them of their commitment to God. The ring is a visual reality check when they consider losing their virginity in the heat of the moment. If we need visual reminders about people we see almost every day, imagine how much more we need tangible markers for our faith.

> Pass on before the ark of Yahweh your God into mid-Jordan, and each of you take one stone on his shoulder, matching the number of the tribes of Israel, to make a memorial of this in your midst; for when in days to come your children ask you, "What do these stones mean for you?", you will tell them, "The waters of the Jordan separated in front of the ark of the covenant of Yahweh, and when it crossed the Jordan, the waters of the river vanished. These stones are an everlasting reminder of this to the Israelites." (Joshua 4:5–7 TJB)

Our #1 Visual Aid

God instructs us to establish anchors, everlasting reminders of His miraculous care. He wants our children to ask, "What does that sign mean?" The most powerful concrete reminder God has given us is His written Word, a book that we can read and touch. While there are over two hundred references in Scripture about music-making, there are over fourteen hundred references about writing and words. Why is the written word so powerful? Why would God choose this medium to reach us?

> In the beginning was the Word, and the Word was with God, and the Word was God.
>
> John 1:1 NIV

The written word is life changing because it is permanent. Legal documents are binding because they are written and signed. Knowing that their name has been written in the book of life is one of the most comforting thoughts for believers. Daniel 12:1 states that when the distress of the end times comes, we will be spared because our names are written in the book. God tells us: "See, I have engraved you on the palms of my hands" (Isaiah 49:16 NIV).

> I will put my law in their minds and write it on their hearts. I will be their God, and they will be my people.
>
> Jeremiah 31:33b NIV

God intends the written word to be His most significant visual reminder: "Keep the pieces of wood you have written on in your hand where they can see, and say, 'The Lord Yahweh says this: I am going to take the sons of Israel from the nations where they have gone. I shall gather them together from everywhere and bring them home to their own soil'" (Ezekiel 37:20–22 TJB).

These concrete reminders are meant to be woven into our daily lives, being a constant witness to our families:

> You shall love Yahweh your God with all your heart, with all your soul, with all your strength. Let these words I urge on you today be written on your heart. You shall repeat them to your children and say them over to them whether at rest in your house or walking abroad, at your lying down or at your rising; you shall fasten them on your hand as a sign and on your forehead as a circlet; you shall write them on the doorposts of your house and on your gates. (Deuteronomy 6:5–9 TJB)

While the Scriptures are God's love letters to us, we are called to be God's love letter to the world: "You yourselves are our letter, written on our hearts, known and read by everybody. You show that you are a letter from Christ, the result of our ministry, written not with ink but with the Spirit of the living God, not on tablets of stone but on tablets of human hearts" (2 Corinthians 3:2–3 NIV).

Moses may have inscribed God's word on tablets, but our hearts are inscribed with God's truth through Jesus Christ. Jeremiah prophesied: "Deep within them I will plant my Law, writing it on their hearts. Then I will be their God and they shall be my people. There will be no further need for neighbor to try to teach neighbor, or brother to say to brother, 'Learn to know Yahweh!' No, they will all know me . . . I will forgive their iniquity and never call their sin to mind" (Jeremiah 31:33–4 TJB).

Holy Words

> When you speak, your words echo only across the room or down the hall. But when you write, your words echo down the ages.
>
> —Bud Gardner

Survival step #12 is to embrace concrete reminders of God's care, especially His written word. Make a conscious effort to weave those reminders throughout your day. After the Israelites were victorious over the Amalekites, God told Moses in Exodus 17:14 (TJB): "Write this action down in a book to keep the memory of it." Many believers still do this today. They use journals to communicate with God, respond to His Word, and record ways that God has miraculously cared for them. It becomes a permanent document. When facing a difficult time, people read these journal entries to remind and encourage them that God will remain faithful. They write down specific Scripture passages that are helpful and comforting. The word *journal* is derived from the same root word as *journey*.

Elizabeth Dewberry describes encountering God through writing as an act of worship and prayer. She explains that words are holy: "Through words you can actually communicate with God. That's powerful stuff for a writer." Henri Nouwen kept a secret journal that he credited with helping him survive deep despair, depression, and suicidal thoughts. Years later he agreed to publish his journal, titled *The Inner Voice of Love*, to help others fight despair. This book was distributed to bookstores on the day of his funeral. Writing is as powerful a weapon as music-making. Through published works or private journals, countless writers have found healing from grief, abuse, or other pain. Often a work that began in private misery became publishable in later years.

It shouldn't surprise you that God the Creator is a musician, an artist, and a writer, and He communicates with us through those mediums. The goal of every concrete reminder is to help us remember Him and what He has accomplished for us, not only yesterday or ten years ago, but for future eternity. These reminders are signposts along our journey so we don't become lost or confused with detours.

> Writing is a friend whose shoulder we can cry on. Writing is a confidant who listens and lets us sort things out. Writing is a comrade, marching with us through the steep days of sorrow and despair.
>
> —Julia Cameron

Pain Clinic

- As a Suzuki teacher, I believe that talent is a myth. God would not command us to pursue activities (like making music) that we are incapable of learning. Every human being can participate in making music, creating art, writing, and dancing before the Lord. These are His gifts to us. Look for ways to focus on God through integrating music, art, movement, and writing experiences into your life.

- Reflect on the power of the written word. Hebrews 4:12–13 tells us that the Word of God is alive and active. It sifts the purposes and thoughts of the heart. How has God's Word been a living tool in your life? When has it comforted you, challenged you, guided you, and directed your life in other ways?

- Think of mini-experiences that you can weave into your daily life, especially on difficult days when your thorns seem overwhelming. Use God's weapons.

> Many writers come to their craft only after they have been shattered by life in some way.
>
> —Christopher Vogler

A friend is a loving companion at all times,
and a brother is born to share troubles.

Proverbs 17:17 NEB

The Christ in a friend is stronger than the Christ in us and strengthens the Christ in us. When Christ is the source and center of a friendship, forces to pull us apart are impotent.

—Lloyd Ogilvie

While efficiency and control are the great aspirations of our society, the loneliness, isolation, lack of friendship and intimacy, boredom, feelings of emptiness and depression, and a deep sense of uselessness fill the hearts of millions of people in our success-oriented world.

—Henri Nouwen

Lifelines 18

My lot is more bitter than yours, because the Lord has been against me.

Ruth 1:13 NEB

In the Old Testament book of Ruth, Naomi's husband has died, leaving her with two sons and their wives. Then both of Naomi's sons die, and she realizes that she will soon be destitute. Naomi tells her daughters-in-law that she is too old to marry again and bear more sons for them to marry, and they should return to their mothers' homes. They are young enough to remarry. As they weep, Naomi tells them, "No, no, my daughters, my lot is more bitter than yours, because the Lord has been against me" (Ruth 1:13 NEB). One daughter-in-law, Orpah, returns home, but Ruth, also a grieving widow, refuses to abandon Naomi: "Where you go, I will go, and where you stay, I will stay. Your people shall be my people, and your God my God. Where you die, I will die, and there I will be buried. I swear a solemn oath before the Lord your God: nothing but death shall divide us" (Ruth 1:16–17 NEB).

Jonathan is equally devoted to David (1 Samuel 19:1–2). Jonathan defies his father, Saul, to protect David. He is loyal to David until his death. Jonathan is David's lifeline.

> David was afraid because Saul had mounted an expedition to take his life. At that time he was at Horesh in the wilderness of Ziph. Jonathan son of Saul set off and went to David at Horesh and encouraged him in the name of God. "Have no fear," he told him, "for the hand of my father Saul will not reach you; you are the one who is to reign over Israel, and I shall be second to you. Saul my father is himself aware of this." And the two made a pact in the presence of Yahweh. (1 Samuel 23:15–18 TJB)

Jonathan travels to give David courage. He sacrifices for David. They make a pact before God, just as Ruth swore an oath to God. Jonathan and Ruth made these commitments for a lifetime. When David learns of Jonathan's death, he mourns:

> O Jonathan, in your death I am stricken,
> I am desolate for you, Jonathan my brother.
> Very dear to me you were,
> your love to me more wonderful
> than the love of a woman. (2 Samuel 1:26 TJB)

Ruth and Jonathan led challenging lives, sacrificing rightful positions to stand by Naomi and David. God intends for us to be in deep, intimate relationships with other people. Are you privileged to have a Ruth or Jonathan in your life, someone who will stand by you, no matter what life brings? More important, are you a Ruth or Jonathan in someone else's life? While we may have many friends, we will probably only have a few of these committed lifeline relationships. We seem to know when God directs us to care for specific people at this depth. Ruth and Jonathan suffered with their own pain and thorns, yet they devoted their lives to easing the pain of Naomi and David.

These lifetime relationships are gifts from God, especially helpful when we feel, like Naomi, that the Lord is against us (Ruth 1:14). When Orpah left, Ruth clung to Naomi (Ruth 1:14 TJB). Some people have described these lifelines as "Jesus with skin on." Ideally, some of these supportive lifetime relationships are in our family, perhaps a spouse or other relative. Yet many people who live with thorns do not have these family relationships. Often difficult family members are the root of their thorns. ***Survival step #13*** is to embrace deep, intimate, committed lifeline relationships. Appreciate and recognize the Jonathan or Ruth that God has brought into your life, and be sensitive to God's calling to make the same investment in someone else's life.

After Marie's husband divorced her and Lori's husband died after a lengthy illness, these two women became each other's support system. As in Marie and Lori's experience, our lifeline relationships are often mutual, but it is not guaranteed that our lifelines will work out this way. Sometimes we are Ruth or Jonathan to someone who does not have the emotional resources to reciprocate our care.

Micah 2:7b (NEB) states, "Does not good come of the Lord's words? He is the upright man's best friend." In Exodus 33:11, Moses spoke to God face to face, as a friend. God is our ultimate best friend. Yet when our pain makes it hard to feel God's presence, He will often send an actual person, touched by His spirit, to cling to us and not let go. Initially, Job's friends were his lifeline.

Job's Lifelines

> Silent comforters are the true mediators of God.
>
> —Barbara Brown Taylor

The book of Job is a textbook for what to do and what not to do in helping a struggling person. Job's friends were solidly supportive during the beginning of Job's troubles. They traveled to be with him. They wept and mourned with Job. Job 2:13 (NIV) describes their devotion: "They sat on the ground with him for seven days and seven nights. No one said a word to him, because they saw how great his suffering was."

Anyone who has experienced great pain, such as losing a loved one, experiencing a divorce, or even being fired from a job, will tell you that most friends are supportive during the initial crisis, but few friends remain faithful for the long haul. They tire of the crisis or don't know how to help. Job's friends, who originally practiced compassionate silence, soon grew impatient and began advising and confronting Job. Barbara Brown Taylor says this about Job's friends: "They are in God's way. They are trying to insert themselves between the silence of God and the one for whom the silence is intended, and in the end their interpretations are more painful to Job than the silence itself."

In Job 6:14 (NEB), Job states: "Devotion is due from his friends to one who despairs and loses faith in the Almighty." When we are struggling with God is when we most need faithful friends. Yet many Christians are uncomfortable with those struggles, do not want to listen to someone doubt or question God, and choose to separate themselves. Lauren, whose teenage daughter became pregnant, and Emily, who didn't know that her son was gay until he contracted AIDS, found many Christians in their church community unable to offer support or even say kind words of comfort. Jennifer received little support when her son was murdered because he had been involved in criminal activities. Christians today say as cruel things to each other as Job's friends said to him. In my observation, these thoughtless remarks are usually made by people who are unfamiliar with suffering. God did bring people into Lauren's, Emily's, and Jennifer's lives that had been through similar experiences with their children and expertly comforted and guided them.

Parents of special needs children have sometimes shared with me how difficult it is to know that their children will never mature into independent adults. These parents will always be ultimately responsible for their care, and they will probably not attend their children's college graduations or weddings. When one mother's Down syndrome son did not survive heart surgery, a well-meaning friend told her, "It's probably for the best. Your life will be better off. God knows." The friend's implication was that the Down syndrome boy's life was insignificant, and God was doing this mother a favor. The grieving mother wondered how her friend would feel if her son had died after surgery. Would she feel better off?

Fair Weather Friends

In the final chapter of Job, God restores Job's life in abundance. Now his friends and family, who abandoned and betrayed him during the crisis, return to be part of his new life. God says that Job's friends did not speak properly about Him, as Job had done (Job 42:8b–9a). Job even prayed for God to spare his friends' lives, practicing forgiveness.

> Yahweh restored Job's fortunes, *because he had prayed for his friends*. More than that, Yahweh gave him double what he had before. And all his brothers and all his sisters and all his friends of former times came to

> see him and sat down at table with him. They showed him every sympathy, and comforted him for all the evils Yahweh had inflicted on him. Each of them gave him a silver coin, and each a gold ring. (Job 42:10–12a TJB, emphasis added)

With the crisis passed and Job prosperous again, Job's former friends and siblings come to offer sympathy and comfort, bearing gifts. Most of us know who our fair weather friends are and who our true loyal friends are. Job did not have one friend or family member who stood by to encourage and comfort him during his intense suffering. They returned after his suffering. Yet Job ended up being the lifeline for his friends. Psalm 55:12–14 (NEB) says that it is easier to endure betrayal by an enemy than a friend, especially a fellow believer:

> It was no enemy that taunted me, or I should have avoided him;
> no adversary that treated me with scorn, or I should have kept out of his way.
> It was you, a man of my own sort, my comrade, my own dear friend,
> with whom I kept pleasant company in the house of God.

A Loyal Lifeline

This woman explains how her sister-in-law, a family member as well as friend, became her lifeline, her faithful support through difficult times:

> I was barely twenty years old when I married my husband. I had deceived myself into thinking I was in love, but I quickly found out that I didn't have a clue about love. I didn't particularly like or love my husband. As life circumstances brought more pressure to bear on my soul, I gave my life

to Jesus Christ at age twenty-two. Instead of life becoming better, it became more intolerable. I realized that seriously studying God's Word was the missing element in my spiritual life. I began attending Bible Study Fellowship, where I formed some of the first real friendships I ever had.

Our marriage continued to deteriorate. We had every imaginable problem—financial, relational, physical, and family problems. We still have those problems thirty-five years later, with sometimes more intense seasons of stress than others. But through His Word and Spirit, God has provided respite.

I have five precious sisters-in-law and a large, caring extended family. My husband has become a comfort to me, now that I understand true unconditional love. Yet one sister-in-law, Diane, has been an angel. Married to my husband's brother, she understands our familial problems and how our husbands were raised. She has her own marriage challenges, though they are different from ours. While Diane has not lived with the serious financial issues that my husband and I have experienced, she has often felt emotionally abandoned and known poverty in a different way.

Diane and I have prayed for each other, commiserated, and encouraged one another for the past thirty-five years. We have been able to vent, knowing what we say is kept in complete confidence and our families will not suffer for it. One day she called me, and I began to sob so hard that I couldn't talk. She simply started praying for me. We never judge each other's husbands. We know that they're not perfect, but we are not perfect either. Diane lives in another state, so whenever I have needed a retreat, I could travel to visit her and also see my nieces and nephews.

Even though we have been financially strapped, God has provided other respites. My cousin annually takes me to

> New York to see the latest Broadway shows and to San Francisco to see ballet performances. We have been guests on several cruises and at vacation resorts. Some people would say that we are lucky. But I know that God is saying, "I am here. I haven't forgotten you. I know you are suffering. I will provide." I no longer give in to worry, panic, or depression. I know that I can trust God. He continues to provide for us, often in abundance.

Just as marriage is often God's most efficient tool for developing Christlike character, the greatest benefit of experiencing thorns is participating in God's most elite training program for developing compassion. We have been selected for this ministry. The word *compassion* means "with suffering" or, an even better translation, "together suffering." No substitute exists for knowing someone who understands your pain because he or she has also personally experienced it. For example, Compassionate Friends is an organization that connects parents who have lost children with other grieving parents. Family and friends can certainly care and try to help, but they will never comprehend the depth of such pain. As one parent who lost a child decades ago told a mother whose grief was fresh, "You need to know that you'll never get over this and that's okay. The scar will heal, but it will always be there. You don't have to explain it to anyone or pretend you aren't grieving as the years pass." This young mother needed to hear those words from another grieving mother, as friends were pressuring her to return to a "normal" life.

Only with the comfort God gives us are we able to comfort others. That is the miraculous chain of compassion (2 Corinthians 1:3–5). Lloyd Ogilvie said that sympathy is concern at a distance, but empathy is true mercy, actually feeling what another person feels. When we have the gift of mercy, we have the ability to feel another person's pain.

> God comforts us not to make us comfortable but to make us comforters.
>
> —John Henry Jowett

Pain Clinic

- Read 2 Corinthians 1:3–5. Where are you in God's chain of compassion? Think about how compassion and suffering are intertwined. Can you have one without the other?

- Ponder the lifeline relationships in your life versus fair weather friends. Who has been your Ruth or Jonathan? To whom have you been Ruth or Jonathan?

- In his essay, "Friendship," Ralph Waldo Emerson wrote, "I do not wish to treat friendships daintily, but with roughest courage. When they are real, they are not glass threads or frostwork, but the solidest thing we know. The two requirements for lasting friendship are truth and tenderness." Think about your most solid, courageous friendships. How did you integrate honesty and tenderness? One without the other does not make for a lasting relationship.

> Compassion, which is the very life of God within us, comes through a slow and often difficult metamorphosis deep within the human soul. It happens through a process. If we look closely at the workings of creation, we find that God always works through process.
>
> —Sue Monk Kidd

Character is not made in a crisis. It is only exhibited.

—Robert Freeman

There is a real pain in your heart, a pain that truly belongs to you. You know that you cannot avoid, ignore, or repress it. It is this pain that reveals to you how you are called to live in solidarity with the broken human race.

—Henri Nouwen

The world breaks everyone and afterward many are strong at the broken places.

—Ernest Hemingway

what do we do with our pain?

19

Anyone God uses significantly is always deeply wounded.

—Brennan Manning

With our final chapters, we now come to the most meaningful part of living with thorns. Our compassion training has led to action. To this point, we have been finding a way to live with our thorns and survive them, realizing that God is saving us through them. We are experiencing a deeper miracle than what is visibly observed. One definition of survival is to live on after facing death. The word *survival* has negative connotations in our culture. *Survival* implies barely making it through life, as opposed to thriving.

But survival can be a celebration. We have defied spiritual death by clinging to God's saving power. We have defied multiple losses and the death of personal longings and dreams to follow God with our whole heart. We begin to see that God can actually enhance our lives through unwanted circumstances. Perhaps when our life journey nears an end, we will reflect, "I would not have chosen it any other way."

Many people find the key to living with thorns lies in transforming their pain by helping others with similar pain. This is a complex process and does not happen overnight. Some thorns survivors reach out to help and walk beside one other fellow sufferer, while others organize movements to help thousands. They are passionate about protecting others from the pain they have known. They choose to be proactive instead of reactive or paralyzed.

Many thorns survivors remember making a conscious decision to change the way they view their unchanged circumstances. They could remain mired in quicksand, or they could move forward with purpose and develop new life ministries. In *Courage and Calling*, Gordon Smith says that our spiritual gifts and God's calling can stay intact, no matter what circumstances we face, whether we are patients in a hospital or prisoners in a concentration camp. ***Survival step #14*** is to transform your thorns by helping others who experience your pain. Christ entered our suffering to heal us. This is our biblical model.

Transforming Pain

> Who can take away suffering without entering it?
>
> —Henri Nouwen

We cannot choose our thorns, but we can choose how to live with them. Melanie is wheelchair bound and lives each day in excruciating pain, yet she travels to the local hospital to counsel other chronic pain patients, just as invalid Amy Carmichael wrote books from her bed to encourage other ill people. Sarah was unable to have her own biological children, so she began taking care of foster children fifty years ago. She is now eighty-two years old and receives cards and gifts on Mother's Day from over 150 former foster children. Bill Milliken was a struggling student who dropped out of school. As an adult, he started working with at-risk teens through Young Life. He founded Communities in Schools, a national organization dedicated to mentoring struggling high school students, helping them stay in school until graduation. Jesse is a former gang member who now counsels teenagers on probation for gang involvement.

Mother's Day is a difficult day for Karen, who lost her only child to cystic fibrosis. She helps raise money for cystic fibrosis research through a Mother's Day fund-raising event. Karen and her husband, David, started an annual scholarship fund in their daughter's honor. They also continue to open their home to their daughter's former friends and remain involved in their lives. They treat these teenagers like family. They help other terminally ill children through Make-a-Wish Foundation. They are determined to keep their daughter's legacy meaningful.

After being estranged from her son for years, Barbara Johnson founded Spatula Ministries to help support other parents of gay children. When Ben's son died as a victim of street violence, Ben established a foundation in his son's honor to create a community center and provide programs for violent teenagers and gang members. After Alice and Leo discovered their murdered daughter in her apartment, they spent months in recovery and then began leading a chapter of Parents of Murdered Children, reaching out to other traumatized families. Candy Lightner founded Mothers

Against Drunk Driving after her daughter was killed by a repeat drunk driving offender. She was soon joined by Cindy Lamb, whose daughter was left a quadriplegic after an accident with a drunk driver.

Beyond Abuse

> Instead of giving up, keep giving out.
>
> —Barbara Johnson

Pam was once a battered wife who kept her husband's secret, but today she runs a shelter for battered wives and speaks about domestic violence at conferences. Amber was once ashamed to tell anyone that she was sexually violated as a child, but today she gives workshops for other wounded women. Many victims of childhood abuse have found healing in writing books or speaking about their experiences to other abuse victims. Alyssa grew up in an abusive home, and her teachers at school were her lifelines. They educated her and encouraged her to pursue her dreams and attend college. Today she is a teacher, focused on helping other children who suffer neglect or abuse at home.

For years Tammy could not even tell her closest friends that her husband was a sex addict. She now leads a support group for wives of recovering sex addicts. Many recovering alcoholics, gamblers, drug, or sex addicts have found purpose and accountability through helping others recover from similar addictions.

Stephanie grew up with an alcoholic father who had rages. He always worked but had trouble keeping jobs because his temper would flare. After Stephanie left for college, she realized that her father was an alcoholic. She hated him and began the hard work of forgiving him. Stephanie became a teacher. She met and married her husband, who was also a teacher. When Stephanie stayed home to mother their four children, she and her husband began opening their home to people in need. For thirty years they provided a safe haven for aging sick relatives, recovering drug addicts, children of drug addicts, foster children, victims of childhood abuse, and others suffering from mental illness. These people lived with them for weeks, months, or years and were expected to follow reasonable rules. If the rules were broken, they would be asked to leave.

Some might say that Stephanie exhibits the classic trait of adult children of alcoholics: the desire to rescue others. Stephanie believes this ministry to the unlovable is a calling from God, a common vision she shares with her husband. Because no one rescued her as a child, she is sensitive to the needs of people affected by addiction. Her own children have thrived and grown up learning to minister to others in need. She modeled a generous heart for them.

Taking Action

Debbie Smith lobbied for Matt's Law after her son died in a college fraternity hazing incident. Megan's Law resulted when another grieving mother testified before state legislators after her daughter was killed by a neighbor. Many current laws and organizations that we take for granted are the result of people taking action after suffering great pain and their devoted efforts to prevent heartache for others. They would say that they do not want any parent to go through what they experienced.

Are there any thorns that God cannot use? Of course not. One former prostitute and recovering heroin addict returned to school and completed her doctorate in AIDS research. She created a mission to protect prostitutes and porn actors—who will not listen to people without experience in the sex industry—from AIDS and other sexually transmitted disease. One former stripper, who became a promiscuous teenager after being raped, leads a ministry to preach the gospel to other strippers and sex workers.

These are just a few examples of the countless stories I've heard through the years about ordinary people who make the extraordinary decision to trust God with their pain. Our ministry begins when we make our own wounds available as a source of healing to others. Henri Nouwen calls us to be wounded healers.

While some thorns survivors organize national movements, others are the "first ones at the scene." When they learn of a crisis, they are the first responders, "spiritual paramedics." Whether they are widows or widowers, parents of deceased children, parents of teen drug addicts, or women who have been abused or violated, these wounded healers who have lived through a specific crisis know exactly what the person in crisis needs to hear (or not hear) and what actions he or she should take (or not take). Spiritual paramedics come to ease a pain they know too well.

When we reach out to help others who struggle, our suffering comes full circle. Our thorns have anointed us with purpose.

> We must bleed to bless.
>
> —John Henry Jowett

Pain Clinic

- Take stock of the thorns you have lived with or currently live with. Think of specific ways that you can help others who also live with that pain.

- Are there ways that you can prevent that pain from affecting other lives? In what crisis are you equipped to be a first responder?

- Throughout the Gospels, Jesus takes action because He is moved by compassion. In Mark 1:41, Jesus is "filled with compassion" and heals a man suffering from leprosy. Jesus also feeds the crowds who follow Him because He has compassion for them (Mark 8:2). Reflect on how your compassion for hurting people is a powerful mirror of the living Christ.

> If you have any encouragement from being united with Christ, if any comfort from his love, if any fellowship with the Spirit, if any tenderness and compassion, then make my joy complete by being like-minded, having the same love, being one in spirit and purpose. (Philippians 2:1–2 NIV)

His (Jesus') appearance in our midst has made it undeniably clear that changing the human heart and changing human society are not separate tasks, but are as interconnected as the two beams of the cross.

—Henri Nouwen

Today, if I had to answer this question, "Where is God when it hurts?" in a single sentence, I would make that sentence another question: "Where is the church when it hurts?"

—Philip Yancey

It is a profound gift to share another person's suffering, simply to be there, willing to blend your tears with theirs.

—Sue Monk Kidd

In closing: The secret

On the last day, Jesus will look us over, not for medals, diplomas, or honors, but for scars.

Brennan Manning

Jesus had scars. Our high priest, who personally understands our suffering (Hebrews 4:15), retained His scars when He returned to earth after His resurrection. Jesus could have been completely healed, but His scars were important evidence for the disciples. Thomas was not with the disciples when Jesus first showed them the scars in His hands and side, where He had been pierced. Upon hearing that Jesus was alive, Thomas said, "Unless I see the nail marks in his hands and put my finger where the nails were, and put my hand into his side, I will not believe it" (John 20:25b NIV). A week later Jesus stood among the disciples again and told Thomas,

"Put your finger here; see my hands. Reach out your hand and put it into my side. Stop doubting and believe" (John 20:27 NIV).

Jesus wanted His disciples to see and touch His scars. In Luke's account (24:39–43), after "show and tell," Jesus asks the most amazing question: "Do you have anything here to eat?" Our Lord is hungry. He is fully human and divine. Jesus understands us at our core, all our wants and longings. His arms are the ones we can run to when we struggle.

Today our scars are important in witnessing to a broken world. We cannot effectively demonstrate God's miraculous saving power unless we are willing to be vulnerable and show others our scars. All the contributors in this book were willing to show you their scars, hoping that their experiences with thorns would encourage and comfort you.

Affliction Transcended

Lamentations 3:32–33 (NIV) tells us that God is compassionate and does not willingly afflict or grieve man. Job 36:15 (NIV) states: "But those who suffer he delivers in their suffering; he speaks to them in their affliction."

We must remember that sometimes we are delivered from suffering, and other times we are delivered through suffering. God speaks to us in our affliction. Jesus helps us meet our test of suffering because He passed through it himself (Hebrews 2:18). Thorns survivors know that perseverance leads to maturity. Thorns produce mature wisdom (James 1:4–5). While we may feel that we lack everything, James tells us that we will be mature and complete, not lacking anything. We are completed by our thorns.

Henri Nouwen encourages us to live through our wounds. Margaret Clarkson said that our faith does not change our circumstances of suffering but transcends them. The survival steps presented in this book will not change our painful life challenges, but they may help us transcend them. Here's a review of the survival steps for living with thorns.

Final Pain Clinic: Survival Steps for Living with Thorns

1. Mourn and seek God.
2. Trust that God will rebuild your life.
3. Engage in honest communication with God, pouring out your heart.
4. Be open to God's honesty with you, immersing yourself in the entirety of Scripture.
5. Align your visions and goals with God's visions and goals.
6. Understand your family's thorns, but also understand that you are not imprisoned by them. Follow God with your whole heart.
7. Practice daily forgiveness.
8. Forgive yourself.
9. Tame your monsters of envy, resentment, and bitterness.
10. Take godly care of yourself and find true rest.
11. Make music to God. Pamper yourself with this gift.
12. Embrace concrete reminders of God's care, especially His written Word.
13. Invest in deep and intimate lifeline relationships.
14. Transform your thorns by helping others who experience your pain.

We can survive our thorns. In the end, our thorn is the miracle that God uses to rescue us. We can follow these steps as we walk a long, steady path that God gives us in His Word. These steps are intended to support us in the daily process of clinging to Him for a lifetime; they are not a formulaic method for eliminating our challenges. The preceding survival steps lead to our final step. ***Survival step #15*** is to grasp the secret of contentment in all circumstances, which Paul describes in Philippians 4:12–13 (NIV): "I know what it is to be in need, and I know what it is to have plenty. I have learned the secret of being content in any and every situation, whether well fed or hungry, whether living in plenty or in want. I can do everything through him who gives me strength."

Contentment and happiness are quite different states. Contentment is being satisfied. God gives us the secret to contentment, not happiness. Happiness is solely based on our circumstances, while contentment transcends our circumstances. We can have the deep anchor of contentment in our soul, remaining unaffected by earthly events.

Jesus had wounds and scars, just as we do. His scars provided our salvation. Our scars come from the thorns we live with. Brennan Manning is right. When we meet our Lord face to face in eternity, He will be looking for our scars. Being a thorns survivor is our painful privilege.

Your crown of thorns will be replaced with a victor's crown.

> Blessed is the man who perseveres under trial, because when he has stood the test, he will receive the crown of life that God has promised to those who love him.
>
> —James 1:12 NIV

Be joyful always; pray continually; give thanks in all circumstances, for this is God's will for you in Christ Jesus.

1 Thessalonians 5:16–18 NIV

It is often out of the brokenness of our lives that God reveals his choicest beauty and blessing. He makes of our tears a rainbow, of our thorns a crown, and of our dark nights a path upon which his love shines with an uncommon radiance.

—Henry Gariepy

He who is able to bring forth rose from brier is able to make the thorn of your hedge blossom and bring forth fruit.

—Margaret Clarkson

References

Quotations in this book come from the following sources:

Albom, Mitch. *The Five People You Meet in Heaven*. New York: Hyperion Books, 2003.

Bonhoeffer, Dietrich. *The Cost of Discipleship*. New York: Macmillan, 1959.

Boyd, Gregory. *Is God to Blame?* Downers Grove, Illinois: InterVarsity Press, 2003.

Brueggemann, Walter. *The Psalms and the Life of Faith*. Minneapolis, Minnesota: Fortress Press, 1995.

Buechner, Frederick. *Telling Secrets*. New York: Harper Collins, 1991.

Cameron, Julia. *The Right to Write: An Invitation to the Writing Life*. New York: Tarcher/Putnam Publications, 1988.

Clarkson, Margaret. *Grace Grows Best in Winter*. Grand Rapids, Michigan: Zondervan, 1972.

Davis, Verdell. *Riches Stored in Secret Places*. Dallas, Texas: Word Publishing, 1994.

Desai, Swathi. In *Something That Matters*, edited by E. Fishel and T. Hinte. Oakland, California: Harwood Press, 2007.

Dewberry, Elizabeth. In *Fiction and Faith*, edited by Dale Brown. Grand Rapids, Michigan: Wm. Eerdmans, 1997.

Diamant, Anita. *The Red Tent*. New York: St. Martin's Press, 1997.

Edwards, Kim. *The Memory Keeper's Daughter*. New York: Viking Books, 2005.

Eldredge, John and Stasi. *Captivating*. Nashville, Tennessee: Thomas Nelson, 2005.

Elliot, Elisabeth. *A Path through Suffering*. Ann Arbor, Michigan: Servant Books, 1990.

Ezell, Lee. *The Missing Piece*. Ann Arbor, Michigan: Vine Books, 1992.

Gariepy, Henry. *Songs in the Night*. Grand Rapids, Michigan: Wm. Eerdmans, 1996.

Haugen, Gary. "When the Will of God Is Scary." *Fuller Focus Magazine* 15.1 (2007): 31.

Johnson, Barbara. In *Boundless Love*, edited by Traci Mullins. Grand Rapids, Michigan: Zondervan, 2001.

Keller, Helen. *The Story of My Life*. New York: Penguin Putnam, 1988.

Kidd, Sue Monk. *Firstlight*. New York: Guideposts Books, 2006.

Kreeft, Peter. *Making Sense Out of Suffering*. Ann Arbor, Michigan: Servant Books, 1986.

Labberton, Mark. *The Dangerous Act of Worship*. Downers Grove, Illinois: InterVarsity Press, 2007.

Lynch, Chuck. *I Should Forgive But . . .* Nashville, Tennessee: Thomas Nelson Publishers, 1998.

Manning, Brennan. *Ruthless Trust*. New York: HarperCollins, 2000.

Nouwen, Henri. *In the Name of Jesus*. New York: Crossroad Publishers, 1989.

_____. *The Inner Voice of Love*. New York: Doubleday, 1996.

_____. *The Wounded Healer*. New York: Doubleday, 1979.

Ogilvie, Lloyd. *The Beauty of Friendship*. Irvine, California: Harvest House Publishers, 1980.

Pipher, Mary. *Writing to Change the World*. New York: Riverhead Books, 2006.

Rivers, Francine. *Leota's Garden*. Carol Stream, Illinois: Tyndale House, 1999.

Rubietta, Jane. *Grace Points*. Downers Grove, Illinois, InterVarsity Press, 2004.

Rutlen, Carmen R. *Dancing Naked . . . in Fuzzy Red Slippers*. Fort Bragg, California: Cypress House, 2004.

Smedes, Lewis. *Forgive and Forget*. San Francisco: Harper & Row, 1984.

Smith, Gordon T. *Courage and Calling*. Downers Grove, Illinois: InterVarsity Press, 1999.

Tada, Joni Eareckson. "Joni's Song– A Song from a Wheelchair," as quoted in *Songs in the Night* by Henry Gariepy. Grand Rapids, Michigan: Wm. Eerdmans, 1996.

Taylor, Barbara Brown. *When God Is Silent*. Boston, Massachusetts: Cowley Publications, 1998.

White, John. *Daring to Draw Near*. Downers Grove, Illinois: InterVarsity Press, 1977.

Yancey, Philip. *What's So Amazing about Grace?* Grand Rapids, Michigan: Zondervan, 1997.

_____. *Where Is God When It Hurts?* Grand Rapids, Michigan: Zondervan, 1990.

other Books by Mary Ann Froehlich:

An Early Journey Home: Helping Families Work through the Loss of a Child

Music Therapy with Hospitalized Children: A Creative Arts Child Life Approach

What to Do When You Don't Know What to Say *

Facing the Empty Nest: Avoiding a Midlife Meltdown When Your Child Leaves Home

Holding Down the Fort: Help and Encouragement for Wives Whose Husbands Travel *

What to Do When You Don't Know What to Say to Your Own Family *

101 Ideas for Piano Group Class: Building an Inclusive Music Community for Students of All Ages and Abilities

Nurturing the WRITE Relationship: Developing a Family Writing Lifestyle and Traditions

Music Education in the Christian Home

What's a Smart Woman Like You Doing in a Place Like This?

*coauthored with PeggySue Wells

About the Author

Mary Ann Froehlich is a music therapist-board certified and Suzuki music teacher. She and her husband, John, have three children. Mary Ann has worked in hospitals, schools, churches, and private practice. She has written articles, music, and eleven books. She has a doctorate in music from the University of Southern California and an MA from Fuller Theological Seminary.

Note to the Reader

The publisher invites you to share your response to the message of this book by writing:

Discovery House Publishers
P.O. Box 3566
Grand Rapids, MI 49501
USA

For information about other Discovery House books, music, or videos, contact us at the same address or call 1-800-653-8333. Find us on the Internet at http://www.dhp.org or send e-mail to books@dhp.org.